The Lost Boyz

A Dark Side of Graffiti

Justin Rollins

The Lost Boyz
A Dark Side of Graffiti
Justin Rollins

ISBN 9781904380 672 (Paperback)
ISBN 9781906162 014 (e-book)

Published 2011 by
Waterside Press Ltd.
Sherfield Gables
Sherfield on Loddon
Hook
Hampshire
United Kingdon RG27 0JG

Telephone
+44(0)1256 882250
Low cost UK landline calls
0845 2300 733
E-mail
enquiries@watersidepress.co.uk
Online catalogue
WatersidePress.co.uk

Cataloguing-In publication data A catalogue record can be obtained from the
British Library.

Cover design
© 2011 Waterside Press. Main image based
on an illustration by the author. Design by
www.gibgob.com.

UK distributor
Gardners Books, 1 Whittle Drive, East-
bourne, East Sussex, BN23 6QH.
Tel: +44 (0)1323 521777;
sales@gardners.com; www.gardners.com

North American distributor
International Specialized Book Services
(ISBS), 920 NE 58th Ave, Suite 300, Port-
land, Oregon, 97213, USA.
Tel: 1 800 944 6190 Fax: 1 503 280 8832;
orders@isbs.com; www.isbs.com

Printed by
MPG-Biddles Ltd, Kings Lynn.

e-book
The Lost Boyz is available as an ebook (see
ISBN above) and also to subscribers of
Myilibrary and Dawsonera.

The Lost Boyz

A Dark Side of Graffiti

Justin Rollins

Foreword Noel 'Razor' Smith

 WATERSIDE PRESS

CONTENTS

Dedication

For my daughter Gabriella

ACKNOWLEDGEMENTS

My special thanks go to Noel 'Razor' Smith my mentor and friend.

They also go to Bryan Gibson for believing in my work.

I must mention each of the following and thank them for their support:

Tony Wood (who has always been like a brother to me); my mother Jane Fall (especially for having me back through the rough times): my big sister Jemma Rollins; Tracy O'Nicolls; Rachel O'Rourke and Bob Stevens.

Other people who have had a positive influence on me during some hard times and played a significant role in helping me to arrive at where I am today include:

Lewis and Jaya Bates; Alice Brooks and her family; Dell Turner, Carl 'Flatter' Latter, Kerry Latter and other cousins; Gary Fall (the only man I would ever call 'Dad'); Auntie Sharon Rollins; Nan Joan Rollins; Tony and Angie Egan and all my other aunts and family; London's Big Dog Hyper (He knows who he is!); David Rubie, Mitchell and Co solicitors, especially Michael Carpenter; Joe Smith's mother Denise and family; Owen Smith; Patrick Grant; Adam Joshua; Fab Mafia Ben'adir; Daniel Campbell; James Byrne; Dagz; Claudia Robinson; Jason Rogers; Sean McGirr; Gary Guilfoyle (a real diamond); Peter Pink and everyone from the Pink's Gym crew; all Warriorz who stayed true and have clean hearts; Tabernacle and Lapa of Who Kares and all of the 'old school' Morden, Mitcham and Sutton boys.

Finally, I should draw attention to the fact that out of respect for certain people some details in this book have been changed.

Justin Rollins
January 2011

FOREWORD

I first met Justin Rollins back in 2001, when he was being held in a top-security cage at HM Prison Highdown in Surrey. He was a skinny, suicidal, messed-up kid with a terrible past and not much hope for the future. His best friend (my youngest son, Joseph) had just been found dead in suspicious circumstances, and Justin was facing a lengthy prison sentence for crimes committed during one of his periods of 'madness'.

Born into a racially-mixed family (his father was Asian and his mother white) and growing up in a predominantly white area of Surrey, Justin was to experience racism as soon as he was old enough to attend nursery school. At an early age his father abandoned the family and Justin's mother had to go out to work, leaving him in the care of childminders who abused him both mentally and physically. Prone to panic attacks and feelings of paranoia he became convinced that he was seriously mentally ill. At school it was made clear to him that he was different and the abuse he suffered because of the colour of his skin only served to alienate him further.

Justin decided to take to the streets. He ran away from home for the first time at the age of eleven and slept rough in a bus station. The police eventually found him and returned him home, but his feelings of not really belonging anywhere grew stronger and Justin was to run away from home many times. Living on the streets took its toll on his already fragile mental health and crime became the by-product of his chaotic lifestyle. Stealing food, and then alcohol in order to numb his feelings, led to more serious crimes. By his teens he had already accumulated a long criminal record and was well-known to the police. At fifteen he was sent to Feltham Young Offender Institution for a robbery that had been committed when he was fourteen.

Justin was one of the growing number of disaffected and alienated youths, drifting through a decaying urban landscape with no ambition other than to leave some kind of mark on the world before checking out for good. He became a criminal not through any desire to get rich or become a 'gangster', but because he so easily slipped through the cracks of a society that, mainly through the influence of the tabloid media, was quick to demonise the young as predators and 'lawless hoodies'.

Nobody thought Justin would live much past his teens. And it seemed as though no-one really cared either way. He sought out other youths in the same position and with the same outlook on life and they formed a gang. Tagging—spray painting their gang name and individual nicknames, or tags, became their main occupation, along with shoplifting and street robberies. This led to more trouble with the police and an eventual four year prison sentence for a attack with a meat cleaver on a complete stranger during an attempted robbery gone wrong.

On many occasions Justin thought about taking, or attempted to take, his own life. As members of his gang either died or ended up in prison, for many years his already bleak outlook on life hardened still further. At the age of seventeen he found himself on suicide watch held in a top security cage in an adult prison. His only companion, in the next door cage, was an infamous murderer who had decapitated and mutilated his victim. For Justin something had to change.

The Lost Boyz documents Justin's road to change and redemption. This is a story of almost feral youths spraying their mark on the urban chaos of pre-millennium London. It is an account of what it's like to grow up as a confused and mentally unstable child of mixed race in a predominantly white area. It is also a tale of mental torture, racism and extreme violence. *The Lost Boyz* takes the reader through the dirty back streets and dark alleys of south-London where vicious gangs of graffiti-taggers fought an all-out turf war that left many victims and casualties in its wake. The lost boys of the title squandered their youth in a nihilistic rush towards oblivion. And some did not survive the journey. Justin Rollins was one of the lucky ones. He spent years in prison before managing to wrest back some control over his life.

Now in his mid-twenties, Justin Rollins is a changed man, hardly recognisable as the youth I first met–physically or mentally. He has a young daughter of his own and is reconciled with the family he once felt so distant from. He no longer drinks or takes drugs, and nor does he see himself as separate from the rest of society. In writing this book, which was a long and painful journey for him, Justin hopes to lay his ghosts of the past to rest. And if it serves as a warning to even one kid who may be starting out on the same road, then it is a job well done.

Noel 'Razor' Smith

October 2010

ABOUT THE AUTHOR

Justin Rollins grew up in south-London where as a youngster he found himself on the wrong side of the law as a graffiti-writer and tearaway. *The Lost
Boyz* describes how his life descended into one of inter-gang rivalry, leading
to violence, other crimes and eventually a substantial custodial sentence for
a robbery on the London Underground. Eventually, therapy and his own
determination led to him turning his life around. Now in his twenties, he
works as a security guard and seeks to discourage young people from making similar mistakes.

THE FOREWORD

Noel 'Razor' Smith is the best-selling author of *A Few Kind Words and a
Loaded Gun: The Autobiography of a Career Criminal* (Penguin, 2005) and
works for the prison newspaper *Inside Time*.

In memory of

Joseph 'Baf' Smith (1982-2001)

Michael 'Vibe' Tait (1984-2002)

Lloyd Lilley (1987-2008)

Jamie Davis (1982-2009)

CHAPTER 1

BORN AND BRED

I was born in 1960s. In those days you could leave your front door open. If you got up to any mischief the local beat bobby would give you a clip around the ear and you would be sent on your way. Only pulling your leg! I was born in 1980s, you couldn't leave your front door open for a second, but if the local bobby caught you up to no good you would still probably get a good beating.

That makes me just twenty-four-years-old as I write this. So, you might be thinking, 'What has someone as young as me got to say that is worth hearing?' Well I do believe I have a quite unique story to tell. Firstly, one of racism. Yeah, I'm the racist one. Nah, I aint really, me next door neighbour's black, so how can I be? Have you heard those kind of lines before? Like me sister is with a Pakistani geezer, yeah he's from Mumbai and I love a Bombay potato, how can I be racist …?!

So my story is in fact one of racism, bullying, mental health problems, the prison system and about how these cold London streets will snatch your life away. It also concerns how a criminal mind can start to develop in childhood and how bloody hard it is after that to break the cycle. I could easily be dead right now, or doing triple life for murder. I've come a long way from walking around my cell tapping things five times. 'If you don't tap that wall five times you're going to die,' my mind was telling me, or 'You can't watch channel five. If you do you will have a heart attack and die right here in your cell all on your own.' I would tap the wall five times. Or I would reply to the voice in my head, 'But please mate, it's my favourite programme is "Home and Away".' But I was still too superstitious to watch it.

That there is known as severe obsessive compulsive disorder. I've also suffered from severe paranoia at times.

'Excuse me bruv, you haven't got a spare Rizla have you?'

'No I haven't.'

So I'm laying there in my cell needing a roll-up thinking, 'Why wouldn't he give me a measly Rizla, it's a small, thin piece of paper for fuck's sake'.

Deep in thought I would figure out that it just didn't make sense.

'He must not like me. Was it that joke I told him the other day, he must have taken it the wrong way? Shit I think he wants to fight me. He is gonna get me, he just is. He is going to stab me'.

Continuing to argue with myself inside my head I would reply, 'Fuck off, fuck off, he ain't, he's my mate' and my mind would reply, 'Come on, if he was your mate he would have given you two bloody Rizlas … He must want to fight me, fuck it. I have to attack him first'.

I was losing my mind and there you have a loose cannon, a nut job, a loon, a bloody handsome loon, called Justin Rollins. I'm gonna take you to every corner of where these mental health problems came from and tell you how I eventually fought back and became a level-headed, nice sort of bloke.

I was born on the sunny side of Surrey in Epsom General Hospital. It was 1984. What can I tell you about good old 1984? The pop star Prince released Purple Rain, the album which would propel him to superstardom. The United Kingdom agreed to hand over Hong Kong. Then there was the Brighton hotel bombing by the IRA, which Margaret Thatcher had only just left before the bomb shredded the middle of the place. Shame that. You're thinking, 'Shame what?'. Shame the bomb went off or shame Maggie had just left? I will leave you to work that out for yourself!

I came out of me old dear a bit of a dodgy colour. Well it seemed to be dodgy in those days. I was brown and all her other babies were white. My mum's father was of Anglo-Indian stock and her own mother, my good old nan, was white-British. This made my mum mixed race, with a slight tan, so that it hardly showed at all and she passed as white. My dad's father was mixed Burmese and French and his mother came from Sri Lanka, a strict Catholic type of woman. So that made me an Anglo-Sri-Lankan-English-gentlemen-skinhead-geeza who could count up to five in French.

I also have an older sister Jemma. Our mum and dad split further back than I can remember. I do know my mother wanted better things from life and she wasn't going to get it from him. So she decided to go it alone. My father didn't try very hard to stay in contact. I hate it when a man says he's done all he can to see his kids. This man never did. No birthday cards, no

nothing. What a coward. He knew where we were, but never even bothered.

My mother was the second youngest of four sisters. They were all given English first names: Sharon, Natalie, Jane (my mother) and Mandy Rollins. My nan's name is Joan Rollins. She also adopted her nephew Tony who I call my uncle. They all grew up in a big house in Worcester Park in a real family home. My mum was the only sister to have children with an Asian man. All my aunties have had white kids, leaving me and my sister as the odd ones out. There are well over a dozen of us who are first cousins. For a short time me and Jemma lived at my nan's house until my mother was eligible for a council property. We soon got moved to a three bedroom flat on the Ben-hill Estate in Sutton, Surrey. My mother found a new partner, a white man named Gary, and though I never called him 'Dad' he's the only man I would ever class as my father.

We still had massive family get togethers at my nan's house. One boiling hot summer's day all of us toddlers were playing in the garden, digging holes and getting dirty. My mum and Gary were heading over to Gary's mother's house, and I was nagging them to take me with them so I was soon sitting in the car for the short journey to my step-nan Jean's house. Gary had what you call a man's best friend, a massive Doberman dog called Brek. This dog had never shown aggression before, but Gary did warn me to stop throwing my ball near to it. As most kids don't listen, I kept on doing it and BANG it happened, my head was in the dog's mouth. Now as a little kid you are not aware of how dangerous some dogs can be.

Ever since then I have known that Dobermans are not so friendly. The Doberman Pinscher was developed by a skilled dog breeder by the name of Herr Louis Doberman in the late-1800s in a town called Apolda in Germany. Having his own dangerous jobs of taxman and night watchman, Herr Doberman set out to breed a medium sized dog that he could train so that it would have the ability to protect him while he carried out his daily duties. The Doberman is a descendant of the Rottweiler and Great Dane. You may wonder why I'm giving you the history of this breed. It is because I see its bite mark across my head every day in the mirror.

So there I am, just relaxing with my feet up, with my head in Brek's mouth and him trying to kill me. By the time Gary rushes over and breaks me free, I am bleeding so much that I soak the whole of the towel wrapped around my head. I received thirty seven stitches on my head and have a nice tooth mark by my left eye. Well, Gary loved his dog and Brek was never put down even though he nearly killed me. Instead, Brek had his big German balls chopped off. I think I'd rather be put down. I do know that in a lot of cases it's the owner's fault that their dog has attacked somebody. But not in my case, Brek just didn't like Asians, the racist bastard.

There you have it, I'm not a big fan of Dobermans and, 'no' I'm not afraid of dogs. I love 'em to bits, especially Pitbulls. They were bred for dog fighting not for attacking humans, but the press loves to brand the Pitbull as a Devil dog. For me they really can be a man's best friend.

As a young child I suffered from a sleeping problem known as rhythmic movement disorder or RMD. This meant that I had to lie on my front with my forehead touching the pillow. I would then quite literally bang my head up and down to get to sleep, sometimes violently. For an outsider looking on in it could be quite disturbing, but I carried on banging my head until I was around thirteen-years-old.

My childhood seemed to be rife with problems. Come to think of it, my life has been. Doctors have always labelled me this or that, or diagnosed me with one thing or another. Like the time I was around four-years-old when I woke up and couldn't even walk. The doctor said it was Guillain Barré Syndrome (pronounced Ghee-Ian Bar-ray). It is a rare but serious disease of the peripheral nervous system, the network of nerves that controls sense and movements. In people with Guillain Barré Syndrome the body's immune system attacks these nerves, causing them to be inflamed, in other words swollen. Inflammation in the peripheral nervous system leads to a tingling, numbing sensation in the arms and legs, but in my case it was just my legs. This can eventually result in short-term loss of feeling and movement, a form of temporary paralysis. As a four-year-old, I didn't walk for a months, I just crawled around one of the Queen Mary Children's Hospital wards playing with my Ghostbuster toys. Come on you're waiting for the next thing to go wrong in my childhood, well wait a minute it's coming-up.

Like I already said, my mum wanted more for herself than living in a council flat, so she started working at Carshalton College doing maintenance work as a painter and decorator. Me and Jemma had started at Manor Park Infant School in Sutton and had been placed at a childminder's flat on the Benhill

Estate. My mum would ride her bicycle the short distance to the college every morning after me and Jemma were dropped at Karen the childminder's place. Now I don't know how the child care system worked back in those days but Karen was not fit to look after children.

Along with me and Jemma was another child called Chris, a special needs boy who had slurry speech although he didn't talk that much. How can I describe Karen? 'Lovely women, just don't let the bitch look after your kids for fuck's sake'. She was, from what I remember, as common as muck. Karen had a few of her own kids as well, so it was quite a busy household. One day her son Peter decided to start strangling me with fishing wire. I was petrified, sweating with fear. He then began to strangle Chris, who just froze. As I said, he never spoke that often. I cried for my mum. Peter was probably about fifteen-years-old, but a nasty little kid. I informed Karen my supposed protector in this environment.

'Stop being a wuss, Chris isn't even crying and he's a spastic,' was her reply.

Now I was a small, five-year-old boy, scared and confused. I informed my mother and she and Karen had words and I don't know what Karen said but I was made to return to her care during my mother's working hours. This I think is where my anxiety started. Who could I turn to now? My mother never helped me. I do not blame her one bit, she was working hard to give me and Jemma a better life. How was she supposed to know I was now having panic attacks? I became withdrawn.

Back at Karen's place the physical abuse stopped but the verbal abuse had only just started. She would tease me and Jemma at meal times pretending we were eating rabbit pie instead of chicken. She seemed to get a kick out of teasing us and seeing our reaction. I remember being locked on the balcony looking down to the walkway below and crying my eyes out. Karen was down there with her daughter tormenting me, calling me a bad loser, and every time they said such things I cried out even more. Karen should have been in the flat with me. I don't know if her hatred was born out of racism or she was just a cold bitch. But when I think back I do have this feeling she was slightly racist. We all have different emotions and handle things differently. This episode may be nothing to some people, but it affected me deeply. I carried that anxiety up into my twenties, along with a fear of institutions of all kinds.

Around this time, I committed a few violent acts on other children, and started stealing things such as toys and money. I was bloody good at stealing and in my teens it earned me a nice bit of money. Karen would drop us off at Manor Park Infants School in the morning and collect us at home time, when I would go back home with a rumbling tummy. Just couldn't wait for that floppy-eared rabbit pie. The violence began one day during art class when for no particular reason I armed myself with a pair of scissors and stabbed a boy in the face with them.

There you have it: the first time I stabbed someone and I was only five-years-old. I don't think the other boy's injuries were too bad. The headteacher along with a couple of other teachers sat me down and started interrogating me about my home life. My face looking to the floor, I froze, became withdrawn and never said a word. This was the same position and frame of mind I carried with me when being questioned all through school, the youth offending programme, on probation and in prison.

I know this violent act stemmed straight from the abuse I was being dished out. Who could I tell though? No-one. I was scared and confused. From this moment on I became a lost boy, a drifter, a tearaway. This was just the beginning of my self-destruction and it shows how delicate a child's mind can be. A child needs to be loved and protected.

Other acts of violence I committed as a five-year-old included hitting two other boys with a piece of brick. Another incident when I acted violently, quite disturbing to think back on, happened when I was hanging around the stairs in my block of flats. There was a deaf and dumb boy who used to run around the estate. He just stared at you making funny noises and waved his hands about. Whilst I was playing on my own by the stairs, the boy approached me mumbling something or other. I decided to grab him and throw him down a short flight of stairs. I stood there for a moment and looked down at him. He was just lying there. I was sure I saw blood, so I ran off and hid in our flat.

When the boy's parents came a-knocking at our door I denied everything and blamed it on the girl who lived next door. I did not feel any satisfaction from committing these acts of violence. In fact they scared me more and more.

I remember another child calling me a 'Paki', so I punched him on his nose until it bled. I didn't know what a Paki was at that age. I was the same as every one else to my mind. My stealing continued as well. When I was stealing at the age of five I would never keep the goods for myself. I always gave them to other kids, even when I stole money from the Christmas Fete I gave it away.

My mum and Gary had now saved enough money to buy their own house, so we were soon on the move again. Yes, no more Karen. Well I say 'Yes', but I don't think I really cared at that stage 'cos my life at Karen's and the abuse I suffered there had become quite normal to me by now. So I left that childminder behind, but the scars came with me to the new place. My anxiety continued and I became more distant from my family. I was in my own world now.

The Lost Boyz

CHAPTER 2

GOING OFF THE RAILS

We soon settled in a three bedroom semi-detached house in Carshalton, Surrey. Me and my sister Jemma attended Hackbridge Junior School. From the word go, I was in trouble for stealing. I denied it of course, rejected accusations completely, and told my mother it was another child.

My mum still worked at the college so I was put into a new childminder's care. The Pescott family lived directly opposite and from what I remember me and Jemma got on fine in their care. Well anything had to be better then being in Karen's care. The thing is, being with a childminder a lot of the time meant not seeing mum too often; only when she came home from work. Then she would be tired, so me and Jem wouldn't get much attention. No one knows the correct way of bringing-up a child in this world. My mum worked bloody hard to put food on the table and keep a roof over our heads, but it seemed all that hard work led to a shortfall in showing us affection. I don't remember her ever coming to pick me up from school. Seeing the other kids with their parents made me quite jealous and feel even more distant from my mum.

At Hackbridge the bullying wasn't long in starting and I was being called a Paki by other kids. Once, whilst having a fight with one of them, his mother shouted out, 'Kick the Paki's head in'. I could feel the hatred in her voice. On another occasion a few kids lit some fireworks and posted them through a neighbour's letter box. Me and Jemma knew nothing of the incident but the word around the local streets amongst the parents was that 'the two Asian kids done it'. We were getting blamed, so we ran back to tell mum.

'Mum, Mum … we're being blamed for setting off fireworks, they're saying we're Asian. What's an Asian?'

I remember having it explained to me that my father's family originally came from Sri Lanka , which made me feel different. I didn't like it. How was I a Paki? My name was Justin Rollins, all my family were white. I felt like an outcast. Around that time Carshalton and Sutton were really racist areas. Asian shopkeepers were terrorised and black kids beaten up. Cars would speed by with someone shouting out 'Paki' or 'nigger'. To put it bluntly, I grew up being ashamed of having Asian blood in me and I believed it was dirty to be a Paki. My mother is extremely light skinned and to this day I class her as a white English woman. And Gary was a pure white Englishman, so to me walking down the road with them it looked like I wasn't their child, like I must have been adopted. I'm sure they got quite a few stares from passers-by. People would say things like that Gary must be a kind man taking on Asian kids. Well fuck me I must have been the only Paki who didn't eat curry and was brought up eating beans on toast!

After I left Karen's place my raw, random violence stopped for a time. I was getting into fights with other kids but not using weapons. Though there were two occasions when I did hurt people with a hammer, both were accidents, 'I swear officer'! They happened in the back garden when me, my sister and a neighbour called Sean put a tent up. I used a club hammer to bang the pegs in to hold the tent upright. Whilst playing in the tent, I decided to leave to get some drinks from the house. I noticed the club hammer on the grass so without thinking I picked it up and for some unknown reason decided to throw it at the tent. I threw it towards the part of the tent which I thought was unoccupied. All I heard was a scream. My sister had moved into the target area and, to be straight, I'm lucky I never killed her. I was petrified waiting for my mum to get home from work and discipline me, so at that tender age I barricaded myself in my bedroom, an act I would repeat years later in prison. I was warned never to play with hammers, but two weeks later we decided to put the tent up again. Messing around, I started to hit the football with the hammer as hard as I could, when all of a sudden the hammer head came off and hit Sean just above the eye. I started to panic and so did he as a bubble the size of a golf ball appeared on his head. Then, just like a balloon popping, it burst and blood sprayed everywhere. Sean wasn't allowed to hang about with me after that.

My destructive behaviour continued. I started to set fires, smash windows and my stealing carried on as well. I began to sneak into the headmaster's office and steal goodies from the lost property box, coming out with the odd watch or ring. That was like gold dust to a ten-year-old. There was a bus stand to the left of my house. I would place my toy cars under the wheels then wait for the bus to leave. I got some sort of satisfaction from seeing the destruction.

When it came to fires, I would set whole fields of dead grass alight. I then stepped up to making petrol bombs. You can see the criminal mind developing, and I was knocking about with other lost kids and we got up to all sorts of things. I was only ten-years-old and truanting from school—and the days when I was in school I would be stealing money from the other kids.

I remember once whilst getting changed for physical education I decided to steal another child's shoe. I thought just taking one shoe would be more amusing than taking both. I walked the fifteen minute journey back to my home, passing the River Wandle on the way, where I took the shoe from my school bag, threw it into the water and watched it float away. The next day sitting in my class the shoe victim appeared at the door and started asking, 'Has anyone seen my shoe?' No-one had a clue it was me and I felt a sort of adrenalin rush. I became an adrenalin junkie throughout my childhood, always going the one step further.

I still never saw my biological father, but on a few occasions I saw his mother. She was a strict woman and quite firm. I didn't like going to her house. It was different, smelt funny and had weird furniture. She and my grandad would take me to museums in London. With them it was no fun, just learning, learning and more learning. I did learn something from one trip to London with them though. Whilst sitting on a train I was glancing out of the window when I noticed a rusty old train parked up along a siding. All of the windows were smashed and it was covered in colourful writing. I asked my grandad what this writing was and he told me it was known as graffiti, an act of vandalism. Wow, this was what I called proper destruction. These guys risked their life to cross these tracks to write their signature. And they did it with style. I wanted a piece of the action and from that day onwards I became a graffiti-writer.

I was ten-years-old, armed with a permanent marker and heading for a white bridge next to the River Wandle. At this stage I didn't have a tag or any sort of signature. I used whatever came into my head such as MFP which stood for Mother Fucking Prostitute. I believe I picked it up from a west coast gangster rap song. And yes, rap music and its violent content does have a negative affect on a youngster's mind. In those days after watching certain music videos I used to want to go out and kill people, like what these rappers rhymed about. If you take away the beat and the rhyming and just say in normal English what one rapper has just said—it could be for example 'I'm going to get my gun, go out and sell drugs, sleep with your girlfriend, then shoot a police officer dead'–then you're telling a young mind listening to that shit all the wrong things. And some people think people are not going to be affected by it!

So now I was a graffiti-writer–a somebody. It was an identity of sorts. Pulling out a pen and leaving my mark on the wall gave me a real buzz . The other graffiti-writers I met were a lot older then me. They taught me how to steal spray paint, which sort of paint was best to steal and where the key places were to write and gain respect from fellow writers. The main place to gain respect and for your name to be noticed was the railway. Our local station was Hackbridge.

I now made up a real tag. My new name was Fes. I remember being eleven-years-old and spraying-up 'Fes' on the wall in a local alley. Next to it I added '1996'. One graffiti act we would carry out was called bushwacking. This meant standing on one station platform waiting for the train to pull up on the opposite one, then jumping down onto the track, running towards the waiting train, crossing the live rail, and spraying our names on the side of the train before it pulled away. I was so small I could only just reach high enough. But what an amazing feeling I got as jumped back up onto the platform and watched the train pull away with Fes written on the side of it. That train was heading right into London for everyone to see.

Hanging around the local station we got talking to the manager, Ruderford Odeye. He was also the manager of several other south-London railway stations. He would preach to us about the dangers of the railway, plus the risks from writing graffiti. Although he never knew what our tags were, he realised we were involved in spoiling his stations. He was a kind man, and would treat us to food in the local café. Another guy would have had us arrested. He always used to say that he just wanted to talk to the graffiti-writers to tell them the dangers of playing on the railway. So I asked him what graffers he wanted to talk to and he spat out some big graffiti names and then also said 'Fes'. I was happy he said my name. This meant I was on the up and all my hard work was paying off.

To really go hard doing graffiti you have to be out at night. The thing here was that mum and Gary never let me stay out all that late. So it was only on the odd occasion that I got to really do some damage. One night I managed to stay out past midnight—I remember I was only eleven. Me and a couple of others boarded a train to Wandsworth Common, walked down the busy railway line towards Clapham Junction and wrote our names wherever we could. Now in the world of a graffiti-writer, this was the type of place you wanted your name to be seen, and there I was aged eleven earning my stripes. There must be around six different tracks to cross around that line and you have to listen so carefully for oncoming trains. Time your run wrong and the Gatwick Express will turn you to mincemeat.

Around this time, I started secondary school. I attended Carshalton High School for Boys. It was bang in the middle of the St Helier Estate, quite a rough sort of establishment and as usual I got into loads of scraps. The pattern was always the same. I was sometimes bullied, I sometimes bullied other people, and I truanted quite often. I made some good friends and had quite a lot of fun the times I was actually there.

Ruderford Adoye attended our school assembly and started preaching about the dangers of the railways, plus about how two boys who he knew attended the school were not big and clever for carrying out vandalism. I thought this situation was pretty funny. Everyone in assembly knew who Ruderford was talking about. I was beginning to get known for being a troublemaker. But my time was coming to an end at Carshalton Boys, since mum and Gary wanted to move yet again. The night before their wedding the house was burgled. The area was a violent one with a lot of burglaries. They had had just about enough of Carshalton, so the next stop was going to be Lower Morden. I wasn't too bothered about leaving. I was being badly bullied around that time and my anxiety was running high, so I was happy to be on the move. In reality, I was running away from things as well.

So my graffiti days went on hold for a while and I started attending youth centres and doing other things. But this mellow time didn't last long. I started having contact with one of my cousins, Tony—or Tone as we sometimes called him—and we were to become more like brothers and get into loads of trouble. At that age we were bad for each other. It was a case of who was the maddest, who would cross whichever line first. We became runaway children, both running from our disturbed childhoods. We were blood, so it made us even closer, and we seemed to be stuck to each other's side. Both of our lives would have taken different directions if we had never formed such a close bond. But it was signed and sealed. It was me and Tone until the end.

CHAPTER 3

THE RAILWAY CHILDREN

Tony was the son of my mother's eldest sister, Sharon. Seen from the outside, his lifestyle and upbringing were not a lot different to mine. People said they could see how he turned out like he did, but could never understand why I was the way I was. Why didn't these people mind their own business?

Sharon suffered from post-natal depression after Tony was born. In those days they just dosed up women with loads of medication, a bit like they sometimes do nowadays. Sharon's mental condition never really got better and years down the line she was diagnosed with mild schizophrenia. Tony grew up believing that his mum was ill because of him—and due to her mental state she sometimes couldn't cope with bringing him up.

Again, from the outside, it looked like I had a happy home and that Tony's was unsettled. Sometimes even he couldn't understand why I had turned out the way I did. As kids we never spoke too deeply about our issues but I'm sure he resented me at times. Yet mine wasn't a stable home. I felt no real connection with my mum or with Gary. The streets were becoming my home.

It seemed that the more I got into trouble, the more I argued with them and in my mind they were 'against me'. So I used to run away. The longest time I was missing for was a couple of weeks, but such periods started to become a regular event. The more I ran away, the more I became distant from them. I would sleep in loads of different places: old cars, parks, train depots. Being on the streets, you were naturally drawn towards other street kids and became friends with them. Whilst doing a bit of graffiti on a train in Chessington, I was caught by two plainclothes officers from the British Transport Police. To be honest they were quite fair and didn't arrest me on the spot. They decided to come to my house a few days later and speak to me there. So one day they turned up at my front door to interview me under caution. Once they had finished, they got talking to my mum and warned her about a couple of brothers who were older than me that I was knocking around with.

I was only twelve-years-old at the time and the brothers were sixteen and seventeen. Kenneth and Keith Gormley were graffiti boys like me, but years ahead of me when it came to drinking and fighting. The officers swore that these guys were *serious trouble* and that they would probably get nicked for murder sooner or later. A few months down the road they were in a fight with a lone man in a park in Sutton. Their victim was badly beaten and left with severe injuries. Keith had already been caught, and now Kenneth was on the run. So the police officers' predictions were half true at least.

I was on the run as well, but only from the family home. Somehow I linked up with Kenneth Gormley, his girl friend Sarah, another girl and a runaway kid called Ian from Wimbledon. That night we were out on the Putney streets pretending to passers-by that we were lost and hungry and we begged enough money to buy some hot food to fill our little bellies. The thing is that, in reality, we were lost as well as hungry. That night we all climbed into Wimbledon Train Depot, found a slam door train and climbed aboard–and that is where we slept for the night. Come three in the morning I should have been in my house fast asleep, then getting up for school the next day. Me and Ian were far from asleep. I had climbed on top of the roof of a carriage armed with a fire extinguisher whilst Ian was on top of the train standing opposite with another one. Let the fight commence: we were running the length of both trains trying to soak each other. This woke up another trespasser, a stinking old tramp who was trying to get to sleep in a neighbouring train. He soon got drenched by the foam.

Morning came and no luxury breakfast was being served in this hotel, so we jumped the fence back out onto the streets and headed off to find something to eat. We soon boarded a District Line tube which was heading towards Upminster in Essex and stayed on board all the way there.

It was Kenneth's idea to go to Essex. I just went with the flow. I'm sure he believed it was quite a lax area that was easy to shoplift in. We must have stuck out like sore thumbs, because after a while we noticed we were being followed. We headed back to the tube station to make our getaway but were quickly rounded-up by the police. I was name-checked and I flagged up as being missing, so I was detained. Next it was Ian's turn. He was ten-years-old yet his mother hadn't even bothered to report that he had disappeared

Then they came to Kenneth. He gave a false name because he was on the run for the brutal attack on the man in the park. But these Essex police officers were on to him. They asked if he had a bulldog tattoo on his left arm and when it was revealed that he did the officer turned around to face him.

'Kenneth Gormley, I'm arresting you on suspicion of attempted murder ... '.

His victim didn't die. He was still lying in a coma and eventually made it through. The officer read out his rights as if he had always wanted to say a line with the word 'murder' in it, but the charge was later dropped to section 18 grievous bodily harm, known as GBH with intent, one of the most serious forms of assault. Keith and Kenneth received quite long prison sentences, although Keith got the lighter one. A few years later, I would be there on the night his actions earned him a life sentence.

When it comes to being reported missing, if the police catch you they have to take you in because you are potentially vulnerable. They would often take you straight home, but I have been held in a police cell and treated like a convicted criminal until someone could come to collect me. Me and Tony handed ourselves in to Sutton Police Station one evening, explaining to the receptionist that we were homeless. We thought our plan would earn us a stay in a children's home together. The plan backfired when we were thrown into the back of a meat wagon for a bumpy ride back home. For the two of us to want to be put into a children's home together must have meant that we were in a dark place for such a young age. When Tony did spend some time in such a home in Surbiton I ran away, climbed into the place and slept in a burnt out room. It truly was a depressing place to get your head down.

Train depots and bus garages were like five star hotels, but some of the places where I slept were almost unbearable. Me and Tony slept in a burnt out, charred van one night. It was so cold we had to hug each other for warmth. Other horrible resting places were the boot of a car and under a bush in a train depot. During my sleep in that bush I was bitten all over by God knows what kind of insects. These days I rest my head in a kingsize bed to make up for all those restless nights on the streets.

I started getting into my graffiti again around this time, and it was the in thing to have a number as well as a tag. It was also time to change my graffiti name. I no longer wanted to be called Fes so my new name became Aliez and my number was 706. I chose the number 706 because other graffiti-writers had smaller numbers such as 59 or 77. The 'writing a number next to your name' phase faded-out quickly for most people but with me it stuck. Then I dropped the Aliez part and became simply 706; the only graffiti-writer in London with a number rather than a name. From the word go, my tag was getting noticed for being different.

Tony's home town was New Malden, so this brought us into contact with graffiti-writers from the Kingston-on-Thames area. I was there on the day a writer named Tabz invented the graffiti gang called WK. WK stood for both 'Who Kares' and 'Wanted Kriminals'. I was invited into the gang. Around that time there were probably twenty writers in the gang putting-up WK on walls, fences and so on. It seems weird now to think of a WK tag next to a 706 tag because the WK writers became my arch-enemies later on. But for now I was part of their gang.

It was spring 1998 and the railway children were born leading to some of the last years of real London graffiti, after that there was no significant competition, not enough talent and most graffiti on the railways was getting cleaned off within days. We lived on those trains that spring writing our tags everywhere. There were plenty of tricks of the trade when it came to leaving your mark. We would go out and steal fifteen millimetre paint pens from art shops, pour out the paint and rinse out the pen. Then we would re-fill the cartridge with shoe dye. It caused real problems for the train cleaners. It was almost impossible to scour off, so that left behind would be a nice big stain.

Writing-up your tag was known as 'taking a bomb' or 'bombing'–or sometimes 'blaming'. Imagine you are on the phone to a friend telling them you're about to bomb a train! If the police got wind of what you were saying you could find yourself nicked under the Terrorism Act ('I swear officer, I'm a graffiti-writer, I don't know a thing about al-Qaeda'). A 'throw up' was the description for a symbol you would paint up, usually a short version of your name. Mine was a big question mark but a number seven at the same time. Other people started to call me Sevens, short for 706.

Now a 'dub' is totally different from a 'bomb'. A dub is writing up your name in bubble or block style. Originally a dub was coloured silver and had a thick black outline. As most black spray paint sinks into a brick wall, we would use wax oil. This stuff just rested on the brick work and left the dub looking big and bold. A 'piece' is similar to a dub, but is usually multi-coloured with fades and patterns.

We railway children always travelled for free, so it was a continual cat-and-mouse game with the ticket inspectors or TIs. Rail maintenance workers in their orange overalls were known as 'trackies'. We would hang out of train windows screaming at them, 'You dirty trackies'. TIs were the graffiti-writers' enemy, even if in reality they were just men trying to feed their families. British Transport Police were our arch-enemies and we would sometimes embellish our tags with 'Fuck BTP'.

I was writing my tag all over south-London and I went about with graffiti-writers from every corner of the city. There were so many writers about that I could board a train to Clapham Junction and meet up with other writers who would be hanging around. The graffiti-writer's sport is train surfing, climbing up onto the back of a train and hanging on as it speeds off to the next station. This is highly dangerous and I would warn any kid not to try it out. Surfing would always be from the back of the train, because if you was surfing the side you could easily be blown off by a passing train.

A fight broke out on a train one evening and these rugby players gave us no chance. We were in for a good beating. I ripped the train doors open and began to surf the side of the train as it sped through the city. These rugby guys were banging on the windows taunting me, and I was hanging on for dear life praying we wouldn't pass another train or I would have been mincemeat. To make matters worse they were trying to poke me through the window with their umbrellas. The train approached Clapham Junction and once it came to a halt I jumped down onto the tracks and ran off.

Another activity we would engage in was breaking into the driver's cabin. We would then get onto the the intercom used for announcements and make our own using the microphone. Everyone sitting on the train would hear this and wonder what the hell was going on. Tony's back garden fronted onto the railway tracks at Malden Manor Station and he had the back bedroom. So there I was sitting in the driver's cabin, with the train coming to a halt at the station. Then I would get on the horn and wake half the neighbourhood up. I was really trying to wake up Tony and it worked. He would be hanging out of his bedroom window waving at me as I was hanging out of the driver's cabin.

These cabins contained boxes of detonators to be laid on the tracks if there was a signal failure and they were designed to let off an almighty bang which would alert the driver to do an emergency stop. They were like fireworks in the hands of a graffiti-writer, but you had to drop heavy rocks onto them for them to explode. The bang was so loud it left you deaf for a few minutes. This once backfired on me when a piece of detonator hit me on the nose, which swelled up to twice normal size.

If we were waiting for a train but it was not going to our chosen destination, or only passing straight through it, we would still board the train, time it correctly as it was heading towards where we wanted to go, then pull the emergency cord. The driver would do an emergency stop, and we would simply rip the doors open, jump down onto the tracks and bang, we had arrived where we wanted to be. It was dangerous but efficient. We railway children knew all the tricks and treated these trains as our homes. For me the railway tracks late at night have always been a place of peace. Put it this way, it is a hidden world, no-one is there except you and the foxes. I would sit on one of the rails drinking a beer looking up at the stars feeling free. I just loved that undiscovered world. You would have to duck down when a train flew past. You could feel the gust of wind as it sped by, towering above. I used to lie as close to the track as possible, feel the ground shake and see sparks fly over my head–but what an adrenalin rush!

The year 1998 was alive with graffiti and trains pulling up with dubs on their sides. I was now famous in the world of graffiti. I was different and I had my number sprayed-up everywhere. Trains were pulling up with 706 across them and by the age of thirteen I was claiming the respect of the older 'all city' writers. Jealousy and racism were in the air and a few WK writers disliked my new found fame, so I started to get bullied by them. They would chase and verbally abuse me, taunting 'You Paki' and all the other shit they came out with. Other graffiti gangs would copy my style of painting so that often you had to look hard to spot the genuine 706s from the fake ones!

One day, I bumped into another boy who was two years older then me. His name was Joe Smith. He was a Morden boy whose tag at that time was Spyer. We got talking, exchanged numbers, then began to write together. After a while, Joe changed his tag to Baf or Bafler. A few other writers from the Morden and Mitcham areas joined us along with Tony and before you knew it a gang was forming. Me and Joe had the same taste in music. We would listen to a group called Bone Thugs In Harmony, especially a track called 'Waste Land Warriorz' which stood out for us. We named our graffiti gang after that track.

So WLZ was our new mob, the Waste Land Warriorz–straight out of Morden. But things move fast in the gang world and WLZ lasted only a few weeks before being shortened to WZ for Warriorz. This was mine and Joe's gang and we could never have imagined it would take off in the way it did. At that time, the biggest graffiti gang was out of north-London, with the most talented and daring writers. It was every graffiti-writer's dream to write for them, except ours. We were to become the most rowdy and violent graffiti gang ever to hit the London streets. Word on the street was that WK were unhappy that our gang had styled itself WZ, because the two sounded similar to each other. Threats were made from their side in an attempt to stop us writing-up WZ. But we weren't going to stop for anyone. The Warriorz were out to play - and although some WK writers had had chased me in the past, they were not going to get away with that any more.

At one stage we could fetch up seventy or so WZ members, a force to be reckoned with. Morden Underground Station was our headquarters, Morden our town and we loved her, so when on home turf WZ also stood for War Zone. The war with WK was about to start and it was all down to one letter in two gangs' initials. It is strange now when I think of how a couple of young boys could start all of the chaos which was to follow.

It was Sevens and Baf from now on and Morden was mine and Joe's. What we thought of as minor crimes of criminal damage like graffiti-writing would lead on to bigger crimes involving violence and dishonesty. That winter I would commit my first street robbery armed with a hacksaw. The following year would bring me a spell in prison aged just fifteen. WZ were turning into a darker, more disturbed gang–and I was right in the thick of it.

CHAPTER 4

RUNAWAYS AND ROBBERIES

When the Warriorz first started, there was me, Joe, Tony and Nemz. The more WZ was being written-up everywhere with spray paint the more we gained respect from other graffiti-writers. It meant that more graffers wanted to join us new kids on the block.

We never exactly chose the town of Morden as our base. But it was central to us all, so it seemed the right spot to hang around. The pluses were that we had a Northern Line tube depot and station right on our doorstep. Morden Station first came into use in 1926 with the opening of the extension of the City and South London Railway line from Clapham Common. Back then it was a rural area and the station was built on open farmland giving its designer, Charles Holden, more space than had been available for the majority of the stations along the new extension to the existing line. The new line became known as the Morden-Edgware line alongside great names such as the Baker Street-Waterloo line which later became the Bakerloo Line. Other names that were made up for the Morden-Edgware line were Edgmor, Mordenware, Medgeway and Edgemorden. It was eventually renamed the Northern Line in 1937. My theory is that because this line had the deepest darkest tunnels on the London Underground it was given the colour black on the tube map. When we first entered Morden the place had never heard of CCTV. It had not seemed like a troublesome town; and since we left it seems to be relatively peaceful once again.

It was now the winter 1998 and I was fourteen. Joe was sixteen and Nemz fifteen. We were all competitive and jealous of each other. I put this down to our ages. We would argue over who was the best graffer and so on. One evening, Nemz and Baf were out with a girl graffiti-writer and a big writer from north-London. The four of them were hanging around a local train station when they spotted two lone teens. One of the four decided to rob these boys, threats were made and the victims handed over their property. None of us had ever been involved in that type of act and it was new to us all. When

I met up with Joe and Nemz the following day they explained what they had done. I felt an amazing adrenalin rush. Joe and Nemz were showing off about the robbery and I wanted a piece of the same action.

We were travelling on a Thameslink train through local stations when we decided to jump off at Sutton Common. The evening began normally and we got up to the same things as usual except that I had one thing on my mind. The Thameslink train stations back then were run down and scary places to be, but they were nothing new to us. I noticed a boy of around the same age as me standing alone by the timetables. I asked him if he had any spare money. He replied, 'No', so I started to threaten him, trying to impress my peers even though Baf and Nemz were telling me to stop.

I thoroughly enjoyed the adrenalin rush and feeling of power but this boy wouldn't hand over his jewellery or money, which was winding me right up right and proper. Joe and Nemz had succeeded at their first attempt and here I was trying to impress them and getting nowhere fast. Suddenly another train started to arrive which calmed the situation for a while. The boy boarded it and so did the three of us. Joe and Nemz thinking that little escapade was over. They sat and spoke to the boy and reassured him everything was now fine. I left them and made my way to the end of the carriage where I broke open the emergency tool cabin and pulled out a hacksaw. I walked back to where my mates and the boy were sitting, pulled out the saw and put it towards my intended victim's face shouting-out, 'Take off your fucking jewellery, now!'. I then told Nemz and Joe to pocket it and jumped off the train at the next stop. We ran along the outside of the train to the middle of the carriage and I pressed the button to lock the doors. These buttons are not for passenger use but strictly for the use of railway staff. With the victim now locked inside the train, we made our getaway throwing away the saw as we went. It was hardly The Great Train Robbery–but it was a start!

So there I was at the age of fourteen committing street robbery armed with a hacksaw. We sold one of the boy's bracelets for pennies, shared the shrapnel and made our own ways home, promising to meet up the next day to sell-off the rest of the boy's belongings. When I arrived home, it dawned on me what I had done. I was extremely confused and worried about my actions. I had never done a robbery before; even the word 'robbery' was scary. As a grown man looking back, I think of how pointless this act was. We didn't exactly make good money and I left a boy shit scared. It was also an extreme form of bullying.

But back then I never thought of such things and even though I was terrified of getting caught it never stopped me from committing other crimes. This robbery cemented my pathway into a life of crime. Fuck me, what am I saying? A life of crime, I'm only in my twenties, I did go on to do more robberies with weapons and like most criminal behaviour it gets worse as it goes along. I ended up using my weapon of choice, a meat cleaver, to cut someone, which I will come to later on. For the time being, I was fourteen-years-old, weighed around six stone and looked a right little weakling.

The next day, me, Joe and Nemz met up as we had two more pieces of jewellery to sell, a necklace and a bracelet. Because Joe was the eldest we agreed he would be the one to try and off-load them at a pawn shop in Sutton. Whilst he was selling the goods, me and Nemz made out we never knew Joe–by just hanging around inside the shop trying not to attract suspicion, wearing hoodies and caps. All of a sudden the guy I robbed entered the shop with his cousin who knew me from school. Fuck, I was in the shit now. Joe abandoned the jewellery and the three of us barged through the door and made our exit. We hit the alleys and disappeared before the boys in blue showed up.

That day we walked around in regret, all of us worried about what was going to come of this situation. Shit, we were going to go to prison, that was what we were telling each other. I nearly collapsed with anxiety and I was shit scared to go home in case the police were there. But eventually I made my way there where I was tip-toeing around mum and Gary hoping they wouldn't find out what I had been up to. I was panicking, just waiting for the doorbell to ring. Every time the phone rang I thought it was the police.

'Ring, ring'–I ran to the phone and a voice on the other end cried out, 'You fucking Paki, you're going to get it, robbing people, you scumbag'. It was the victim, only now he was playing the hard man because he had his friends with him. But don't get me wrong. I thought I was hard at the time. I was threatening him in front of my own friends. Now I knew for sure that the victim had realised who I was and I was in really deep shit. I had to leave the house and hit the streets for the evening. When I returned home later that day the atmosphere felt even more strained and noticeably different. The police had been there looking for me. They had searched my bedroom and told my mum what I had done. She was going mental at me, whilst Gary refused even to speak to me, though his face said it all. My mum told me to get my fucking arse to bed because in the morning she had to miss work to take me to see the British Transport Police at Victoria Station, where I would be questioned by the robbery squad. Fuck me, I was shitting myself. I had a poor night's sleep, woke at seven o'clock and decided to do a runner. As mum and Gary slept, I climbed out of my bedroom window and made my way to cousin Tony's place.

The boy I robbed had gone to the police, but he had also been threatening me on the phone. I don't blame him for threatening me, but if you're going to grass then let the police deal with it. If you're not going to grass and you want to take matters into your own hands then do that. You can't have it both ways. To this day I can't stand grasses, but if you're a do-goody type of guy and you live by those codes then that is your choice. But you can't start to threaten the guy whilst you're prosecuting him as well.

Tony's house was in enemy territory so I had to watch my back. Being on point, means being on the ball and what I've learnt is you can never really be on point twenty-four seven. I was walking along a shortcut to Tony's place when out the corner of my eye I noticed someone running at me. I turned and got knocked to the floor.

'You fucking WZ bastard, you dirty Paki.'

With that I got repeatedly hit around the head with a spray can and kicked by two WK members. I really hated being called a Paki, because these racist mugs actually believed I was different and I was dirty. I believed it too. I was called 'Paki' so many times that I started to hate myself. I thought I *was* dirty and because of this I was becoming ashamed of my Asian roots. I even started to hate Asian people. I was turning very, very angry.

I finally reached my cousin's house and told him I was on the run. We decided we would do a runner together, along with one of Tony's mates. The first thing was that we needed money. We managed to rustle up around fifty quid between the three of us. It was decided that we would run away to Bognor Regis, where, so our foolish young minds had heard, we would get a bed-and-breakfast for the lot of us for forty pounds a night. Who in their right mind, would let three scruffy runaways with fifty quid to share stay in their B&B? Alternatively, we convinced ourselves that we might be able to break into an empty chalet at Butlins. What a perfect plan! In reality, it looked like we would end up sleeping on the beach. Nonetheless, we headed off, believing that we would be gone for weeks and have the time of our lives.

By the time we arrived in Bognor it was evening, freezing cold and there wasn't one B&B that hadn't closed for the winter. All we could do was find some type of shelter in which to sleep. We bumped into a couple of local girls and told them of our predicament. They informed us that if we gave one of their mates 'a little change' he might let us stay at his home.

We made our way with the girls to their friend's house and were introduced to Magic Man Dan who had a dog called Domino and who said that for ten quid we could have a roof over our heads at his place. The magic man was a white hippy with dreadlocks and his dog a mongrel. We gave the girls a bit of money and they left to go and buy us some cannabis. They too could have done a runner, but in fact they returned with the goods. Magic Man Dan's friend turned up, a man by the name of Patrick. We all sat in the front room of Dan's home smoking and talking. As the cannabis took hold of my young mind the night seemed to get weirder and weirder. Magic Man Dan put on his strobe lights and a reggae beat while Patrick started singing the sweetest reggae songs you will ever hear. While all of this was happening, Domino the dog was barking and the magic man was doing some weird slow dancing in time to the music. It turned out that Patrick was originally from Morden and we knew a few of the same people.

The night got weirder by the minute and I soon passed out. I woke in the morning and didn't have a clue where I was, panicking initially. But Magic Man Dan appeared and told me Tony and his mate were in the next room. I woke them up, we said our goodbyes, made our thankyous and left. Our holiday was over down in Bognor and we bunked the train all the way home. Well I say all the way home, but I didn't have a home to go to now. If I returned there, I would get nicked, so that option was out of the window. From then on, I began to get used to the fact that I never really had a place to call home, a place of security, a place where I could rest my head knowing that when I woke up I would have nothing much to worry about.

Tony's friend decided to go home, so now it was just me and him left.

We decided to put up a tent in Tony's back garden as his mum didn't want us staying in the house. It was absolutely freezing outside, so we decided to put on all of Tony's clothes for warmth and by the time we were finished we looked like we were two Michelin Men. We thought it hilarious, and it went on for several days until Tony's step-dad, Vincent got fed up with the both of us. The final straw was when Vincent caught Tony pissing up the side of the house while I was laughing my head off because the clothes Tony was wearing made him look so fat. Vincent never saw the funny side of it and we were soon on the move again. Tony was on the move because his home life was unstable. The two of us needed each other through these times and we seemed to make each other laugh, sometimes quite mentally, and we still do so today.

The daytimes were now spent shoplifting for food and spray paint; the night-times searching for shelter. This one evening we were planning to sleep in the Wimbledon train depot. We climbed in in the usual way and made our way onto a slam door train. We headed into a first class compartment and it was so cold we had to rip down the curtains for blankets. We also tore off the silk, pink, head cushion covers to wear as hats since our ears were nearly falling off with frostbite. But the cabin was so cold we decided to find a warmer train. With our pink hats on our heads and the curtains stuffed up our jumpers, we headed off in search of one.

As we walked through the depot we were spotted by a group of trackies, and without a word we legged it in different directions. It must have been a strange sight for those trackies around two in the morning, chasing what looked like two fat kids with pink hats around a train depot. I was running along one side of the train and the trackie was on the other side. I kept looking under the train and seeing his legs. But I soon outran him and managed to climb out of the depot. Tony got caught, the police showed up and they gave him a lift home. As for me, it was a night sleeping on the streets alone.

The next day I met up with a graffiti-writer named Zelda. He was what I'd call a true veteran street kid. He had been living that way for as long as he could remember, but was now staying in a hostel in Leytonstone, east-London. We left Morden Underground Station on the tube and headed to the hostel. I had never been to the area before and felt quite anxious. I had to climb in through the window as he wasn't allowed to have people stopping over. As we were talking away there was a loud bang on the door and I hid in the cupboard. I could hear one of the hostel workers explaining to Zelda that the TV had been stolen from the recreation room.

The worker left and we had to keep the noise down because the hostel was now looking out for a thief. I fell asleep but was woken by another bang on the door, so got back in the cupboard. This time it was the police. Luckily, they never came in to search the room. If they had opened the cupboard door they would have had quite a shock when they found a little Asian tearaway half asleep. We left early in the morning and I was spotted by the hostel worker. He immediately assumed that I must be the TV thief, even though I was so bloody small that I would not have been able to carry it.

We headed towards London Bridge Station. When we arrived there Zelda decided to pull the fire alarms. Bells were ringing all around the place as we ran and boarded the first train, just as the commuters were being evacuated. Luckily our train pulled away and it happened to be heading towards Morden. I later heard that Zelda pulling that alarm caused massive disruption to rail travel at London Bridge all day long.

As the train headed towards Morden, Zelda climbed onto the back to 'skitch' it. I stayed inside until we came towards less busy stations then joined Zelda. We were hanging on, laughing our heads off, passing over railway bridges with members of the public staring-up in amazement. I looked over towards Zelda and he was holding on but leaning as far back as he could so that his body was nearly touching the track as the train speed along. He was in stitches, letting out wild noises. I thought that this must be a new way of surfing, so I got myself in the same position. It was not until I looked up that I saw the train driver in his cabin looking down on us and giving us the 'you're mental' sign. Zelda was having the time of his life until the train started to slow down as it pulled into St Helier Station. As I was on the platform side, I jumped and fell as the train was still moving, rolled along the platform like you see in the movies, got to my feet, caught sight of Zelda–and we both legged it.

Walking through the park opposite to the station we bumped into Joe and his friend Reg. Me and Joe caught up on all of the news about the robbery as we walked towards Morden. Joe's friend, Reg, was known to be a good car thief, and the plan now was to steal a car. Within seconds Zelda and Reg had hotwired a red Ford Escort van. We jumped in the back and sped off on our way.

This was my first experience of joy-riding which I found to give me quite a buzz. We decided to go and steal some cigarettes from a local newsagents, but that plan didn't go so well. Zelda was seen by the staff and arrested by the police. It wasn't long before the police were on our tails as well. A police meat wagon spotted us in the stolen van and a chase started. I've only ever been in one other police chase, when I was driving my own car in my early twenties. I got into a bit of road rage with a guy who kept on cutting me up and as we pulled-up at the lights side-by-side threats were made. I opened up my glove compartment and reached for a hammer, waved it around at him and he turned from hard man to grass. He got on his phone to the police. I didn't have a licence anyway, so blew straight through the red light only to see that he had done the same. I managed to lose him, but was spotted by the police. Their blue light went on and I thought, 'Fuck this', put my foot down and the chase was on with me on the wrong side of the road, winging it though the town until I lost them. What an adrenalin rush. After that I could understand why people stole cars and went joy-riding. I got rid of the hammer and sold the car the next day. I was on my own that day and got myself out of the shit. But the chase I got with Reg and Joe wasn't so good because Reg was in control of my destiny.

The meat wagon was catching us up, so Reg took a sharp right and headed down a dead-end. He crashed the car into a fence alongside the Carshalton Athletic Football Club ground. Game over, we were well and truly nicked. We never had a chance to leg it before we were handcuffed and on our way to Wimbledon Police Station. I had been running from the British Transport Police for around three weeks because of the robbery, but my days as a fugitive were now over for a while. The thing is that the BTP had not put out a warrant for my arrest, so Wimbledon police did not have a clue that I was already wanted.

My mum refused to be an appropriate adult for me whilst I was being interviewed with regard to a charge of taking a conveyance without consent (known as TWC). It was routine, when this happened, to wait for a social worker to accompany any young person who was being interviewed. I was charged with TWC and received a police caution. In the meantime, my mum refused to have me home, so I was put in a foster home for the night in Colliers Wood. In the morning, the foster carer dropped me off at the social services office in Mitcham where I was told to remain in the waiting room for a member of staff to come to see me. I had a good look around then scarpered. That night I decided to turn up at my mum's house for food and shelter. She let me in and I went straight up to bed and a deep sleep.

'BANG, BANG, BANG.'

I could hear the front door. It was six in the morning and I was being rudely awakened by the BTP. I was arrested for the robbery and whisked back to Wimbledon Police Station to be processed. I got the feeling that the Metropolitan Police didn't take too kindly to the BTP monopolising their cells and interview rooms. The officer in charge of my case was one of those evil looking control freaks, his face and grin seeming to glow with delight as he intimidated me. This was the same officer who a friend of mine once overheard saying, 'Yeah it's a shame about these niggers, they hunt in packs', so I didn't expect any favours. I later bumped into Joe and Nemz in the station and they had been arrested for robbery also. I was charged with one count and Joe and Nemz with two each. We were all given bail, mainly because we were still young and had never been convicted before of any violent offences.

A couple of weeks later, we were up in Wimbledon Youth Court and because of the gravity of the offence the case was sent to Kingston Crown Court. We would remain on bail for the next nine months whilst we waited for our case to come up there for trial. Fuck me, I was fourteen-years-old and due up in a Crown Court for a street robbery with a hacksaw. I was one hundred per cent sure that I was going to prison. At that age you believe the stories you hear about what happens there. I had heard that boys get raped in the showers and all sorts of bad things. I now know this is not true, but at that young age you accept such rumours, which I guess are put about by people who have never spent so much as a day in a cell.

The Lost Boyz

CHAPTER 5

MIND GAMES

It was now early-1999 and the WZ boys were out on the street. Word soon spread that me, Joe and Nemz were on bail. This earned us further respect from other kids in the area, even though we were shitting ourselves about the fact that we were going to prison. But we lived up to the hype. We made out that we didn't care and that we were as crazy and bad as everyone was saying we were. This frame of mind seemed to stick with me. My tag was 706 but some kids were calling me Seven o'Sick. However, one way or another I had found my new identity. I was no longer a weak, dirty Paki as I thought I was viewed by some of those who bullied me. I was now a madman. It was a great tactic for keeping people at bay.

There was a group of black boys in the Sutton area who went by the gang name of SK, which stood for Shadow Krew. I knew a few of them pretty well and learned they had problems with WK as we did. SK knew our base was Sainsbury's car park behind Morden tube station and they started to turn up and hang about with us. There was talk of both gangs teaming up to go and catch WK in their own territory of New Malden. I must admit I was a right big mouth at the time and bragged about how I was going to do this and that to WK when I caught them.

A graffiti-writer who went by the name of Lend had moved to the Sutton area from Brixton and in no time he had joined WZ. His school friends from Stockwell also used to come down to Morden by tube to hang about with us. SK was abolished and they all joined WZ so that our gang was now around twenty members strong and pretty multi-cultural. I had some information from a boy who went to school in the New Malden area where WK had a little base to smoke cannabis. So it was time to put this war into action, it was time for me to get my revenge on WK for the times when they used to bully me. Thirty five of us arranged to meet at Morden Station. A younger kid called Crazy Steve from Morden turned up. He was only around twelve-years-old but, believe me, he was a fucking nut job. He brought along with him a homemade weapon consisting of half a broomstick with fifteen screws sticking out of the top side and a Stanley knife blade wedged into the end of it. Though I never knew it at the time, a couple of the Stockwell boys were carrying knives.

Before this episode, there were only minor slanging matches with WK but we were set to make it more personal. We headed on a bus from Morden to Sutton where we had to catch yet another, the 213, which headed to Kingston -upon-Thames via New Malden. At first, when most bus drivers saw us waiting they would put their foot down and drive on past. But we did manage to get one eventually and were on our way. It didn't last long because we noticed a WK boy sitting alone at the front and before you know it he was getting a good seeing to. This delayed our journey as we had to flee the bus, but we soon boarded another. We had just tasted WK blood and now we wanted more.

Now we were in WK territory. The information I had was that there was a long alley which runs alongside New Malden Station. This is where a WK base was supposed to exist. We entered the alleyway and began to arm ourselves. It looked like it was disused, being full of rubbish and overgrown with bushes. This added to the tense atmosphere, where thirty five of us were now creeping along, searching for the base. It was hardly guerrilla warfare. This was urban street war. All of a sudden we came across the place we were looking for. Talk about a dodgy situation. A WK boy who I used to go about with was sitting there. We were still okay with each other up until that point. There were about five WK boys there in total. For a second, everyone froze and then someone shouted, 'Set it Sevens'. The WK boy who I was okay with shouted, 'No Sevens, I'm your mate', but I was with my gang now, a member of the Warriorz and without hesitation I started to beat him with a piece of brick. The rest of WZ followed suit. I remember a vision of one WK member sitting there crying his eyes out as Crazy Steve pulled out his home made weapon and started to beat him with it.

The Stockwell WZ boys started to stab a couple of WK boys in the legs. There seemed to be people running everywhere. Me and Crazy Steve made our exits by climbing through the bushes and over a fence which brought us onto the station platform. We boarded the first train out of there and on the journey Crazy Steve pulled out his tool. There were screws missing and the few that remained had hair and pieces of flesh stuck to them. We all made it back to our base in Morden by different routes where we let out a victory cheer. The battle was over but not the war. It had only just begun.

For a split second the thirty-five or so of us felt like we were all blood brothers, not from our own biological blood, rather from the blood of war, mainly that of our victims. Our attack on WK had been bloody and brutal, but we were kids and at that age you don't seem to have concrete morals. I can't say I planned to make a violent gang, me and Joe just wanted to create one which could challenge other people in the graffiti-writing game. Within days the word had spread through the London graffiti scene that WZ was a force to be reckoned with.

If you take for example a local gang maybe from the local council estate, they may have wars with the boys from other local estates. Both gangs are likely to be known to other gangs in their town or area. But because of our graffiti-writing we liked to travel and spray our tags—and WZ—everywhere we could throughout south-London and other parts of the city. So we were getting recognised all over the place and unlike other local gangs who fought amongst each other on their own patch we got up to all sorts of trouble in different parts of London. I was one of the main leaders, so I was becoming infamous on the grapevine as a violent street kid.

A week or so after our slaying of WK they tried to counter-attack in Morden armed with metal poles and batons, but they were unsuccessful as we were not at our base. So for now it was one nil to WZ

We fought other gangs as well. We would challenge any gang that tried to pass through our territory without invitation. On one occasion some members of another gang tried to pass through, an argument started and we politely asked them to leave. Did we hell, we politely told them to fuck off. One of them replied 'Why should we leave? This town don't belong to you, it's not like your name's written on the wall'. This had us in stitches because everywhere you looked WZ *was* written-up on walls, fences, buses and trains. These guys didn't understand why we were laughing and a fight broke out, but this time it was just fisticuffs and rolling around in the main road in front of the traffic. To a member of the public it may have looked shocking but to us it was just normal behaviour.

New WZ members were joining every week and our gang was involved in more and more battles on the street. We never seemed to lose on our own turf. Me and Joe loved our town of Morden. More then any of the others we classed ourselves as Morden boys. I should explain that WZ wasn't just made up of boys. We had at least five hardcore girl members on our best day. The girls weren't to be messed with either, they were always up for a fight, even with us boys.

Parties were a good place to gain notoriety. Once at one in the Wallington area a fight broke out with a group of Tulse Hill boys. There was about fifteen of our crew and around nine of them. The thing is that half of the WZ members who were there were just followers, they weren't hardcore members out for a rumble. These Tulse Hill boys were rowdy and intimidating, so a fight broke out and they steamed in with bottles. Right in the thick of things was a WZ girl trying to fight them. Even by WZ standards one of the Tulse Hill Boys actions was barbaric. The pretty WZ girl was stabbed in the face with a broken bottle. When the brawl had died down and we all regrouped we didn't exactly lick our wounds and head home. We were all covered in lumps and bumps, but the worst of it was the WZ girl with a nasty stab wound to her pretty face. The Tulse hill boys escaped and we never did manage to exact our revenge on them.

Our gang was no longer just a graffiti gang, it had become a violent street gang and we started to witness these types of brutal acts on a regular basis. We were just school kids aged from twelve to sixteen but we experienced many traumatic events. We handled these childhood scars through alcohol abuse. A lot of us never went home what with stealing food, graffing, drinking and sleeping rough. There might be up to twenty of us bedding-down in a derelict building. I remember lying there on the floor under a table in an old pavilion ready to go to sleep. I looked at my surroundings and saw around twenty of my mates trying to get some rest. Joe was the lucky one who had managed to get a seat on a sofa with a couple of others. I saw Crazy Steve and Tony sitting on a couple of old chairs. I saw the two mixed race twins Snez and Heat on top of a cupboard. Everywhere that you looked someone was taking up a bit of space and making it his or her own. Even at that age I was aware of body language—I could tell the ones who didn't want to be there and I could quickly spot the ones who didn't fit in. They were the kids who huddled together in their nice clothes, who couldn't sleep, who found their surroundings cold and dirty. But to me, Tony and Crazy Steve this place was as about as good as it got.

Looking back, all of the hardcore WZ members had one reason or another for being there. We had all gone through difficult things in our childhoods, which had affected us. These experiences brought us together and our gang was our family. Late at night we would sit high up on the shop rooftops drinking alcohol and watching the world go by. From these rooftops we could hide from the police and watch to see if any of our enemies were on the prowl.

So if you were going home and walking through Morden during the evening in 1999, you may not have realised that the Warriorz were sitting on the roofs above, getting high and expressing their pain through alcohol abuse and madness. If you were picking your nose or scratching your backside we probably saw you and laughed our heads off, so I must thank you for cheering us up through these dark times.

Our gang members were recognised as being the people to be seen with in graffing circles. We had kids from every corner of London writing-up WZ tags, even those from other gangs who would join us for a while. We made our own rules and did it our way, bringing-in writers such as Gusto from Brighton. We would climb into train depots in broad daylight and take liberties. We used those places to chill out and drink as well. Tube depots were different to ordinary train depots. The security was tighter and they had laser beams which would set off an alarm to say there was an intruder. But even these were easy to avoid. First off you had to lay on your front and crawl army style under them–no I'm only winding you up again, you could simply walk around the posts which shone the laser out of them. What a good deterrent hey! I would use the post itself to climb in and out of the depot.

The Northern Line tube trains in those days were the old, dirty, silver ones, and most spray paint stained them. I would use a tin of Plasticote paint called Barbecue Black. The stain this left was awesome. I started to hit the depot so often it wasn't long before I was the most recognised writer on the Northern Line. Nearly every tube that pulled up had a 706 stain on it. These tubes were heading right back to north-London and I gained a lot of respect there from some of the most prolific graffers. But those tubes were so old and dirty that they soon started to get rid of them and London Underground brought in a new model. This was more or less the end of the Northern Line graffiti-writing era, next to my stains on those tubes stood Mefa 95 tags and old school

Chuck tags from the 1980s and early-1990s. Those days were now a memory as these new shiny red, white and blue tubes never held their stain. Nowadays writers have came up with the trick of using spray on paint stripper, so you may have seen tags such as Server and Tox burnt into the blue and red paint—criminal damage at its most creative.

Our gang battles carried on and our territory expanded. Morden was our base, Sutton, Rose Hill, Carshalton, Mitcham, Wimbledon and we shared North Cheam and Raynes Park. I say 'shared' but what I really mean is that those two places were the border which both WZ and WK crossed. WK territory was Worcester Park, New Malden, Norbiton, Malden Manor and Kingston. The Number 213 bus began its journey from Sutton and once it passed North Cheam it went straight through two WK towns on its way to Kingston. I came up with the idea of spraying WZ back to front on the top deck front windows of the bus. So if you were looking up from the outside you would see a massive silver WZ tag. The idea was that when this bus went through their towns they would look up and see our graffiti in their manor. This pissed them off and they started to do the same in return, so that we would look up and see WK written on the front of the bus. All gangs had our own styles of graffiti, ours being more of a London-style whilst amongst my favourite writers from other towns those from Brighton had a weird bubble style.

One night me and Tony jumped into a cab from Sutton to his family home in Malden Manor. We only had enough money to get to a certain point and had to walk the rest of the way which should have taken around ten minutes. It was two in the morning as we were about to pass under a railway bridge to when to my horror I looked up and saw over a dozen WK members. I thought 'Fuck, I've had it here'. They ran down the embankment and couldn't believe their luck. They had the man of the moment right at their mercy. A few punches and I was out cold on the floor. I took a proper beating that day fracturing my ribs and suffering concussion from when they jumped on my head. Luckily a man driving past pulled over and dragged me into his car for safety, and somehow I directed him to Tony's family home. I remember I never even said thank you to that man as I was still seeing stars and couldn't comprehend what was happening. Those WK boys could have killed me there and then. Tony turned up shortly afterwards and swore he couldn't help me as there had been too many WK boys after me. I know he was scared, I was scared too. There were times when I was too scared to help him and vice-versa. We used to slag each other off if one of us ran away, and we were too young to admit it at the time that we were in fact scared.

I got my own back on one of those WK boys one day. This one boy in particular had caused loads of trouble by stirring up things between both sides. If you knew and could feel the abusive phone calls I received from this boy you would understand why I had a particular hatred towards him. My phone would not stop ringing and I was called every word under the sun. I was told evil things were going to happen to my mum and sister. He would even phone me on Christmas Day and scream abuse at me. It gets quite tiring shouting abuse back. If I was with the WZ boys we would all get on the phone and shout abuse. So when I finally caught up with this WK boy I chased him with a meat cleaver. He jumped into a car and tried to escape but the passenger window was open so I ran alongside and chopped him in the cheek bone.

Things were getting out of control, we were treading on a lot of toes and as the saying goes 'there is safety in numbers'. I weighed about seven stone and this reputation I was building for myself always had to be backed up. Because of my size, a bigger kid could easily get me to the ground and believe me I had a few of them on my case. So I used to like to use a weapon to defend or attack, and I found this had a great effect when it came to psychologically breaking my enemies before a fight began. It also sent out a message that I wasn't to be messed with.

I'm not claiming that I was some sort of hard nut, because I was scared a lot of the time and that's why I used a weapon. But over the years things I witnessed definitely made me hard mentally, and believe me there isn't much that will scare or surprise me these days.

There was times when weapons were used on me. One of these springs to mind when we were all out in Streatham and Snez wrote his tag across the side of someone's house. He was spotted by one of the guys who lived in the house who called for reinforcements. We could feel the tension, so decided it was best to scarper. In no time at all they were onto us. I was the only one to be caught and all of my boys disappeared. I got kicked to the floor and beaten with a hammer around my back and legs. It sounds much worse then what it was. I was well enough to escape, and wasn't happy with my mates.

But I knew better then anyone what it was like to be scared.

Another big fight kicked off in North Cheam one evening with a group of men. We were chased into a McDonalds where I jumped straight over the counter so these men wouldn't catch me. All of a sudden Crazy Steve came flying through the window holding a bottle of Archers in one hand and a metal pole in the other. The looks on the faces of the restaurant staff were quite a picture.

Tony came running in and was beaten to the floor. A man started to set about him with a belt which had a massive buckle on the end of it. He was lying there covering his head. I was shitting myself but jumped back over the counter and picked up a metal chair and beat the man over the head with it a few times. I can still picture his face as he turned to look at me. It was pissing blood and he was the image of a scared rabbit. In my crazed state and at that moment I somehow felt on top of the world. I had saved my cousin and it was pats on the back all round for me.

1999 had brought a lot of madness in my life and I hadn't even gone up to the Crown Court for my robbery case. When the time came I pleaded guilty along with Joe and Nemz and in a few weeks time we were up again to be sentenced.

CHAPTER 6

PORRIDGE AND ON THE BUSES

Those nine months on bail passed quickly. I didn't get up to much. You could say that the summer was pretty boring, just a few beatings and gang squabbles but nothing major. The physical bruises soon faded even if the mental scars never will.

In October 1999 me, Joe and Nemz were sentenced to four months each in Feltham Young Offender Institution. I can sit here now and laugh my bloody head off because four months is a matter of weeks, but to a fifteen-year-old boy it felt like a lifetime. Around this time my mother informed me that she and Gary were getting a divorce. I couldn't understand why but I doubt the stress from having me as a son had anything to do with it. To be honest me and Gary never really connected with each other back then, so when I heard the news all I thought was that from now on I wouldn't have to worry about Gary's reaction when I got into trouble. Basically, I did what I wanted to do anyway, but now just living with my mum would be even easier. There would be no rules because my mother could no longer control me. Whilst I was serving my time in Feltham she moved back to Carshalton.

After the judge had finished with me I was escorted down to the cells where I sat biting my nails until the prison van turned up as my anxiety went through the roof. Out in my town I was a nutcase, a kid to be feared. But in here I was a complete nobody. There was every hard kid in from London and beyond. I stood no chance. For the first time in my life I bumped into Asian street kids that were inside for all types of crimes. I couldn't believe my eyes. 'Fuck me,' I thought, 'there's actually hard Asian kids from the ghetto'. Most of them were from east-London. Up until then I believed Asian boys to be wimps due to their lack of response to the racism I had seen as a kid on my local streets. These guys were nothing like the Asian kids I had watched getting beaten up in school. It was a culture shock.

I was the smallest boy in there. I didn't cry the first night but when the situation I was now in finally dawned on me I wept my little Asian eyes out.

(I am laughing to myself as I write this because I'm picturing myself lying in that cell crying, but at the same time that voice in my head would have been saying, 'Get over it you prick, you got yourself in this mess'). I was bullied for my belongings straightaway and was moved to the vulnerable persons unit. I feel no shame in saying this as I was only a small boy living in a rough and different environment. Life on that unit was sweet and comparatively easy. Although it was a traumatic time, I did have some laughs. It was there that I first read a book, which I found in my cell under the cupboard. It was about a man who was lost at sea for weeks on his own in a battered old boat. To feed his hunger he managed to catch a seagull and eat it. I could sense his mental struggle, lonely and on his own. I was in the same position except that seagull wasn't on the Feltham menu, but peacock was.

It was when I started to read my second book in there that I began to hear my own voice slagging me off in my mind. It seems weird to talk about it because this wasn't somebody else's voice, it was mine. It would taunt me, call me a Paki and tell me I was going to die. It freaked me out and once again I started to argue back.

I wasn't forgotten about by the outside world, I was very popular and received loads of letters every day. Some letters were from genuine friends who cared and some were from people who thought it was cool to write to someone in jail. But nonetheless I was happy with the support. My sentence passed quickly and before I knew it I was heading to reception to sign my release papers. Me and Joe got released together, but Nemz had been released two weeks earlier. He still remained in the Warriorz but calmed right down and up until this day has never returned to prison.

For some strange reason, I get the feeling that you lot don't believe that was my last spell in prison. Well you're right there! Did I change? Not one little bit. I still had quite a few years to do in prison, a couple of deaths and some to cope with before I sorted my Asian arse out. Come on, would this book be interesting if I sorted myself out straightaway? Of course not— so don't you sit there wishing I took the right road straightaway. I was stuck in a frame of mind which was my security and my coping mechanism, a complete madman even though I was just a small boy.

Examples of my beginning to get known for being mad were kicking out bus windows, jumping from the top deck, punching my fists into hard objects and smashing bottles over my own head. If somebody wrote their name on a wall five times, then I would write my name on it twenty times. If someone bottled someone, I felt that I wanted to do this twice as many times using a selection of bottles. I became lost in this false personality. All that was ever said to me was, 'You're crazy, you're mad and you're sick'. I didn't know who I was anymore other than that I had a reputation which was growing quickly and that I always had to fight to retain it.

As well as tubes and trains, buses were our second homes. All of the local bus drivers got to know us and they began to hate us. You can understand why. The bus may have just been through the buffer and cleaned at the depot but after thirty of us drunken teens had been on it it looked like a bomb had hit it. There would be graffiti everywhere, our names scratched into the glass windows with tool sharpeners or our names written-up using ice cream or Dairy Lee Dunkers. We would be screaming, arguing and playing our ghetto blasters at full volume. How fucking annoying we must have been! A fight might kick off, windows would get smashed and believe me this happened on a fairly regular basis.

So you would get bus drivers who would see us waiting and put their foot on the accelerator. We would throw things at the bus and shout abuse. One evening I chased a bus that wouldn't stop. I managed to press the 'Open' button on the outside of the doors and tried to climb aboard. The bus driver pressed his button to close the doors, so I fell backwards and my arm got stuck. I was lying out in the street with my arm trapped by the door, but the wanker of a driver put his foot down and I was dragged at thirty miles an hour through the Morden streets. If my arm had come loose I would have gone right under the front wheels. When normal passengers started screaming for the bus driver to stop he did, slowly, and I managed to press the 'Open' button again and climb aboard. I shouted abuse at the driver and yeah you guessed it, I was arrested for fare dodging. No, not really–I was nicked for a public order offence and old *Michael Schumacher* got a pat on the back.

I had only been out of Feltham for a few weeks and the drama continued.

These bus drivers had a real hatred towards us and one day outside Morden station a bus driver hit Joe in the eye with a money tray. Joe's eye was pissing blood. As reinforcements arrived, the bus driver retreated to his cabin inside the bus. With him shielded by glass and plastic he believed he was safe.

But the twins Snez and Heat, who were only thirteen at the time, managed to open the cabin window. I was not there but I watched the CCTV when the boys were up in court for it. I saw one of the twins yanking the driver through the window by his tie and the other punching his lights out. Now as sit here I am laughing to myself, not because I find violence funny, but because it was crazy beyond belief. We were just little kids but these incidents were becoming a regular occurrence. All the boys involved got off with fines and conditional discharges and once again—you guessed it—the driver got off Scot free. He probably even got an award from Transport for London. Believe me, that driver got so much abuse whenever we saw him after that incident.

I once left a bus covered in my own blood. It was literally spraying out of a wound in my right hand. A few WZ boys were at a local party when trouble started with another group of boys from Mitcham. Being in the thick of it, I got hold of a plank of wood, but being the mad boy I now was, I didn't attack the enemy with it, I attacked myself. Yeah, I know, what a fucking weirdo, hey?! So I'm there outside the party screaming abuse at these lads, whilst hitting myself over the head with this plank of wood–and believe me it hurt. I was doing it to intimidate the enemy, to make them think, 'Fuck that, I'm not fighting him, he's a nutter.' So they didn't try to beat me up, they didn't need to, I was doing it on their behalf. I was lucky that there wasn't a nail sticking out of that piece of wood because it would have gone right into my head.

I left the party battered and bruised, boarded a single decker bus alone and took a seat right at the back. A stop down the road a group of five boys were waiting. They boarded the bus and it turned out that they were the group I had had trouble with back at the party. I weighed up my options. I was alone, not tooled-up and had already beaten myself quite badly, so in short I was now well and truly fucked. An argument started and they began giving me a good kicking at the back of the bus. As I tried to stand up I noticed an emergency hammer behind a piece of glass. Aware of the advantages of psychological warfare, my first step was to punch my fist through the glass. The smashing sound shocked them. Next my hand was pissing out blood which I sprayed at them as I hit out with the hammer. In the middle of this fracas, I covered my face with my own blood and let out a war cry. This scared the shit out of them, so I went further, absolutely mental and lashed out with all the energy I could summon. I was now winning this battle and the boys ran for their lives as the bus ground to a halt. I felt on top of the world. I had beaten myself up and come back from a losing position and won against the odds. I sat there for a moment covered in bruises and blood and with this overwhelming feeling of madness deep in my soul.

Those boys never wanted any trouble after that and I still have a piece of glass stuck in my right hand from that night. I was definitely suffering from trauma because of my experience of going to Feltham. I had written to my mum when I was inside promising that I had learned my lesson. But my mum was a stranger to me. I was always out and about and she was going away on holiday with her new partner. So this left me on my own in the new house, which of course I loved. The upstairs neighbours actually moved out because I caused so much trouble, they fucking hated me.

Morden Station was our headquarters and back then only a few of us had mobile phones, so to see if anyone was about everyone would phone one of the four payphones at the station. The phone would ring and someone would answer. It was like our gang's office. We had a few dodgy characters making a home of our office too. At most London Underground stations you get homeless people and tramps. There is a big difference between the two. A tramp would be a smelly old pisshead who did funny things and a homeless person would be more quiet and distant. And as Morden was the last stop on the line you would get all different kinds of characters just hanging about.

Did you know that a man who lived the lifestyle of a tramp used to be called 'a gentleman of the road'? He could be seen with his stick over his shoulder with a bag tied to the end of it. People would stop and stare but respect him — and he was seen as a somewhat mysterious human being back in the late-1800s. Now he's just a dirty old tramp.

One of the regulars was a man we nicknamed Meow. He was a strange character who would lie in the middle of the station forecourt with one hand under his head and his elbow resting on the ground. Then he would simply meow at passers-by. Any normal person would ignore this or might be a little scared of it, but we loved it, it was absolutely mental. Meow had disappeared from the scene, but one day I bumped into him. He was immaculately dressed. I called out to him and asked him what he was up to.

'How come you look so smart, what happened to lying on the floor outside the station?'

'Na, I give it up , it weren't the right career choice,' he replied.

'Fucking mental mate, that's what I say.'

Another guy was your classic tramp. He had one leg and a long grey beard which was stained a yellowish colour. His name was Logan. He loved to drink Tennants Super lager and rant and rave about one thing or another. Whilst talking to somebody on one of the four 'office phones', out of the corner of my eye I noticed a water fountain. I turned around and to my amazement Logan was lying there with his dick out pissing in front of all of the commuters. It wasn't a nice sight. I once nicked a pair of Homer Simpson socks from Woollies and gave Logan one of them for his only foot.

Whilst sitting at Tooting Broadway Station I came up with the idea of making a documentary called 'Wildlife on the Underground' . It would feature the dusty little mice you see running along the rails. Fuck knows what those little bastards eat because there's never anything down there. And it would include flea-ridden pigeons, you know, the ones that can't fly properly–and look like it they are about to hit you so that you have to duck and get all embarrassed. Then there was good old Logan.

I happened to make friends with a tramp from Morden Station. Outside the station I found an unopened can of Fosters lager. I walked up to this tramp and gave it to him and he thanked me and asked what my name was. From that day on I was his best friend. He was around fifty-years-old and a real hardcore alcoholic. His name was Philip but we called him Old Limey after he called someone a limey bastard. I once gave him a graffiti pen when he was pissed out of his head and he proceeded to write WZ all over the place. All joking aside, I cared about Old Limey. I used to sit around the back of the station and drink beers with him — and I gave him a quid or two when I could. He was a nervous man and had been through a lot of rough shit on the streets. He had been sleeping rough for donkeys' years. I think that I was his only mate–and the only person he felt safe with. So I had a go at my mates when they took the piss out of Limey. He would say, 'Sorry Justin' and run off. One day I gave him a full bottle of Teachers whisky. I dread to think about what he got up to after he drank the contents.

When he saw my friends around town he would ask them in his Irish voice 'Where is Justin?' Even when I was away doing time in prisons he would ask after me. It was in 1999 when we formed our friendship and I never really saw him again. In 2005 when my cousin entered Wandsworth Prison he was put in a holding cell in the main reception. He noticed an old tramp sitting in the corner alone and realised it was Limey. He asked him if he remembered the Morden days. My cousin told me Limey was still asking after me and telling him I was his only friend, and he also told my cousin he had nothing left to live for. Old Limey was a broken soul, but I cared about him.

You did get the odd tramp that never fitted in. You had Kestral Head who walked around wearing a Kestral Super lager can as a hat. Tony once had a fight with him next to the open back doors of an ambulance. Tony punched him and he fell straight into the back of the ambulance. What a shot, I thought. You also had Glue Sniffer who would walk around sniffing glue all day–and last but not least you had Morden Morden. We gave him that name as that was all he ever said. Morden Morden was a skinny old Asian man with an evil, scary smile. We were sure he was some kind of pervert. Me and Tony once saw him in Worcester Park and we shouted his name out. He turned round with a sickly smile and said, 'Worcester Park, Worcester Park'. I opened the newspaper one day and read a story of a man who had been found chopped in half and dropped into a Grundon bin. The photograph next to it was of the one and only Morden Morden. And no all of you sickos, he wasn't found in a bin in Morden or in Worcester Park.

As well as tramps there were other types of wildlife in and around Morden. They most probably had mental health problems, but to a kid they were amusing. One of them was Mad Mary. We would call out asking her for the time and she would reply, 'I don't tell boys the time, you are trying to steal my watch, if you ask me again I shall scream'. So naturally we would ask her again and then she would scream the place down. The best time to ask her the time was during the rush hour when all of the commuters were leaving the station. We would ask her in a whisper, then all of a sudden she would let out a loud scream. Most of the commuters would jump back in shock. She never even wore a watch!

The year 1999 was ending and the New Millennium was about to arrive.

There were parties everywhere and the drinks were flowing. For us WZ boys and girls the drink never stopped flowing, we entered a new phase, one that was even more self-destructive. Everyone started to drink more heavily and experiment with recreational drugs such as ecstasy. We would go brew-raising in force. We had a certain way of doing this so as not to raise the suspicions of shop staff. Our method was known as sleeve-raising. First off you needed a baggy coat with elastic around the ends of the sleeves. You would then have your hand hidden in one of the sleeves with just the fingertips and thumb hanging out and with the thumb stretching the elastic to make the sleeve wider. You would then put your arm into the shop fridge and push the can or bottle of beer up the sleeve. Next you would push your hand out so that it appeared as normal and the beer would be safely hidden from view. If a member of the shop staff was watching closely, even he or she wouldn't even notice what you were doing. As hungry kids on the streets we would also use this tactic to steal food, spray paint and pens. One time I sleeved eight Bacardi Breezers, four up each arm. As I left the store a security guard ran out and politely asked if he could search me as a lot of alcohol had just gone missing. I raised both of my arms out in a searching position, the guard then patted-down my pockets and waist down but found nothing. He apologised and left. I left too, but with eight Bacardis up my sleeves. I went and got pissed out of my head.

Even if you were being watched by CCTV operators you could get away with sleeving. You would have to watch the footage in slow motion to see what we were up to. Around twenty of us would go out brew-raising, for us teenagers it was the equivalent of a pub crawl. With it came fights with shopkeepers and believe me there were plenty. I once rode into an off-licence on a mountain bike, pulled up next to the alcohol fridge, sleeved a beer and casually road off into the night. A fight broke out in one Tooting off-licence and ended with Joe serving a short spell in prison. As you know alcohol can be addictive, and with drinking so much and it being free this led to my becoming an alcoholic at the age of fifteen.

With all the madness going on in mine, Joe's and Tony's lives on the streets you can probably understand that alcohol became a coping mechanism. We needed something to help sooth the pain of things we witnessed and things we were going through. Things were about to turn from mad to fucking mental. Crazy Steve didn't have that name for no reason. He was about to destroy our young fragile minds through raising hell. He had discovered a love for the dark arts, Satanism especially.

THE HOUSE OF HORRORS

Crazy Steve was only thirteen-years-old at the time but had the build of a grown man. He towered above me even though I was two years older than him. He was half Irish and half Scottish; in his case something of a fiery mix. I met Steve through my friend Joe, and Steve took a liking to me when he saw my crazy attitude and he became a die-hard member of the Warriorz. He had a reputation of being a wild child so he fitted right in with our mob. He had zero stability in his home life and could do what the hell he wanted from an early age. Irish Brendan was his father, a heavy alcoholic who would always have a can of his favourite cider at the ready. Brendan loved us boys and we were always welcomed into his home. I was particularly fond of him and he was like a father figure to me for a time.

Brendan would always put a roof over my head and cook for me. While all the other boys were getting stoned in Steve's bedroom I would sit with him and talk with him for hours. He would say, 'Look son, you're not like those boys, you're a good lad. Don't you turn out like them'. These were the times when Brendan would stop drinking for a week or two. I'm sure that kept him alive because I doubt his body could handle all that alcohol abuse.

Brendan used to beat Steve as a small child and when I say beat I mean beat with a capital B. His weapon of choice was a snooker cue. He would savagely attack Steve and terrorise him mentally, and without a doubt this affected Steve's mind, and as Steve grew up he became extremely violent himself and showed spells of psychotic behaviour. So by the time he joined WZ he was set to become the most violent of us all. As he had the body of a man you couldn't mess with him and as time went on we witnessed him turning on Brendan, slapping him about and telling Brendan he was now the boy.

WZ started to split up into loads of small groups, and as time went on our friendships with each other seemed to deepen. We were still a big gang but you now had a few different factions. There was me, Joe, cousin Tony, Crazy Steve and a few others. Then you had the Morden white boys and you had all of the WZ black boys, plus you had other kids from in and around Morden. All together we made up the Warriorz.

My part of the gang started to use ecstasy almost every weekend. Most people would use ecstasy to go out to raves, so they could dance for hours and feel totally free and happy. We were too young to go out to raves and took it for the buzz. It gives you such an amazing feeling, all you sense is love when you're on it. But with every up there's a down. The buzz may last for around five hours but the comedown lasts for the next twenty and believe me you feel absolutely like shit afterwards. With the love buzz you actually believe everyone is your friend, very dangerous if you bump into an enemy. Also the lights seem to be blurry, your jaw may be rattling, your eyes can start to close and you might even hallucinate.

We loved the ones that make you hallucinate. I witnessed some weird things whilst on those little pills. They would make you feel so warm and cosy inside, and you could start to hug yourself, rubbing your arms saying, 'This is so good'. One night when I was well away on ecstasy I climbed up under a railway bridge. Have you ever looked under one and seen the piles of bird shit, heaps of the stuff which must have taken maybe ten years to make. Well I climbed up and sat under this arch. I felt so comfortable, my jaw rattling away. I was in Heaven, the best feeling in the bloody world. Yeah you guessed it I was sitting in a mountain of shit talking to myself.

'This is so fucking good, I don't want it to end'.

What a nut job. But can you appreciate the class difference.

'Oh Albert what did you get up to this weekend?'

'Oh I just played polo and took in a spot of pigeon shooting.'

'Oh that's nice. I had the time of my life hugging ten years of droppings.'

Me and my team took everything to the extreme. Whilst high on ecstasy in Steve's room, we would smoke the skunk form of cannabis. There was a dare a lot of smokers would carry out called 'rise and choke'. This meant putting your back against the wall, taking a big pull on a joint, rising up and a friend (a friend he says!) would then strangle you for as long as you could take it. The friend would then let go and you would be gasping for air and literally would be on a different planet–and that is without being on ecstasy. You had to be bloody mad to do a rise and choke, but mad we were.

Sometimes whilst on ecstasy, we would all stand in a row and take a big pull on the joint and strangle ourselves. Once I strangled myself so much I knocked myself clean out and collapsed on the floor. I just lay there for around twenty minutes in Dreamland. This was the start of severe self-destruction. The shit we were doing to our bodies we were lucky we never killed ourselves. Rise and chokes were now a regular thing, originally a triple dare but now the norm. After a rise and choke whilst on ecstasy you felt as if you were on LSD, like you were tripping. Words simply can't explain the type of mind frame it takes to do this. Thinking about it now, it is like a horror movie. It was some scary shit, but we craved more and more of it.

We would climb into graveyards to freak ourselves out whilst on ecstasy, also trek across wasteland and through woods alone. We craved danger and this gave us some sort of sick buzz. We also started to experiment with solvents. They can make you feel quite sick. We would inhale the gas from lighter fluids or certain kind of deodorant. This would produce a dramatic head rush, where the room starts to spin and you have the giggles. Thinking back now that feeling is disgusting and I must have had nil respect for myself because doing solvents means seriously abusing your body. People say there is glamour in cocaine. Well if that is true I can tell you now there is zero glamour in doing solvents. The thing that stopped me doing solvents from age fifteen was seeing a couple of my friends on the bus giggling. They had white deodorant marks all over their sweatshirts from inhaling and this put me off for life.

Drugs can make you do some strange things, but I can't blame the next act fully on drugs even though I'm sure I was on ecstasy at the time. Whilst walking home from Crazy Steve's house in the early hours of the morning, I noticed a dead fox in the road. I carried on walking, but the image of this fox just wouldn't leave my mind. So I walked the short distance back to Mr Foxy and looked down at him where he lay. He seemed so peaceful with fresh blood around his mouth. I then came up with the idea of picking the thing up, no not to hug it! With all of my strength I spun around, threw it in front of a moving car and ran for my life. Now I can blame it on just wanting a hug whilst on my love buzz, but in truth my heart and soul were dedicated to showing every one I was a nutcase. This had a direct link to not knowing who the fuck I was, an Asian-looking boy from a white family, so that my identity was now a madman and it frightened off the bullies. When I told the WZ boys the next day they thought I was crazy and I got proper respect for that.

But someone had to go a step further and yes I'll put my paws up to being envious of Tony for what *he* did. He was walking down the street one fine evening with a few of his mates when he too spotted a dead fox. He picked it up, cradled it like a baby and chased his mates down the road with it, and then holding the tail he swung it at them as they cowered in fear. They were shitting it. It all came to an end when the fox's body separated from the tail and it went flying through the air. He was left holding the tail. At a time when I thought I couldn't get sicker, he stole the show. After that foxes often figured in my dreams and nightmares. The thing is I was doing these crazy things to prove I was nuts, but to actually do them *I must have been nuts*. Whilst I was drunk I would also pick up neighbours' cats and take them home with me which I thought funny. I would wake in the morning to find a big furry cat sitting there staring at me. I also used to steal cats from the local pet shop. I nicked a goldfish once as well by sleeving it, walked outside to Joe and slipped it in his coat pocket. When he looked in his pocket he freaked out and was fuming with me.

I don't remember the first time Crazy Steve started talking about the Devil and it is quite hard to explain how the Devil days started to develop, but I will try my best. Steve seemed to think he was some sort of Devil's servant, that he was in contact with the dark side. With all of us high on ecstasy and cannabis sitting there in Steve's room he would fill our minds with scary tales of how there were evil spirits in the room with us and how he could talk see and talk to them.

This freaked me out to the point where I was petrified. I would have panic attacks believing I was being haunted by evil spirits and so on. Steve's bedroom walls had the odd bit of graffiti on them, but gradually he drew pictures of Devils with horns and hands with eyes in them. Before long the walls were covered in madness. So when you were sitting there high, looking at that shit it would scare us. Steve would also practise his dark arts with the ouija board.

Things went downhill from that time onwards. I was cutting my arms whilst the others followed suit, though maybe not for the same reason. My cutting was a cry for help. But help wasn't coming quickly, it was nowhere to be seen. I remember Joe saying to me 'you don't believe in all the Devil shit do you?' I swept his question aside as quickly as I could. I couldn't exactly tell him I was petrified by it, and that I was so scared I would sleep on my mum's bedroom floor because I was convinced I was going to die.

Strange things started to happen in Steve's room. One night whilst on ecstasy a group of us were in there and one of the boys just burst into tears, then he attacked another boy for no reason at all. The crying boy's face seemed to be glowing. All of a sudden I felt like I was being strangled. I looked over to Steve and he told me there was an evil demon in the room that was trying to kill me, and that the demon was inside the crying boy. I started to see red dots all over the room, my panic attack in full swing. Steve reassured me that his demon was locked in spiritual warfare with the crying boy but was stronger than him causing me to run from the room. That shit was mental. What a head-fuck for a fifteen-year-old.

Steve's room gradually turned from being dirty to disgusting. There were fag butts on the floor, even sick and blood on the walls from all the self-harming. There was talk of Steve and another boy cutting one another and drinking each others' blood. One WZ girl even started to drink from her wounds. Things were bad, real fucking bad. Steve's violence got worse, he was a lover of weapons and was always swinging knives around. By 'accident' he stabbed my friend Verb in the leg. Accident or not, this was nothing compared to some of the other things that happened.

A Morden WZ boy let slip that another WZ boy, Stitch, had hidden a machete behind a row of shops. I marched down there and stole it. No honour amongst thieves—even at that young age. I took it back to Steve's house and handed it to him as a gift. He was the happiest kid alive. He used to be able to swing it at speed using just his fingers. It wasn't too long before he used his gift for real during an argument which broke out between him and his father's drinking partner. Now remember, Steve was only thirteen and his friend's dad was in his forties. Steve retreated to his bedroom only to reappear with his machete, which he swung at his intended victim's head. Luckily the man saw it coming, covered his head with his arms and fell into a cowering position, because otherwise the machete would have gone right through him. Steve chopped into the man's arms, severing tendons and nerves. Somebody then grabbed the machete from Steve, so he picked up a shelf rack and smashed it over the guy's head. It wasn't long before Steve took over that house, and he kicked his dad, Brendan, out. Now it was a Warriorz house.

Even if the bedroom window was closed it would still be cold in Steve's room, which was haunted by evil spirits. He was by now a fully-blown Devil worshipper who believed this gave him evil powers and, to be honest, it did lend him an extra boost of power when it came to violence. We went out on a super brew-raising exercise one time The reason I say 'super' is because we hit around seven different towns getting pissed out of our heads. It was a beautiful day, the sun shining and eventually we were lying in a park in Surbiton in Surrey.

We had to head through WK territory to reach Morden, and as we travelled there we bumped into some WK members, one of these an ex-Warrior, so I asked him why he had switched gangs. Then I decided to punch him right in the face. After a second punch landed he ran for it, around the front of a parked bus and was hit by a car. He looked to be in pain and shock but we never helped him. We just got on the bus and went on with our journey.

Come to think about that incident now, it was quite bad. But to us at the time it was not so unusual. We simply travelled back to our own territory and headed for Steve's place. We were all outside his house when he suddenly came crawling out of it topless, running on all fours like a feral child. This was the first time I had I witnessed anything like this and he was speaking in demonic tongues. He sped around attacking people, growling and mumbling strange words, whilst his face was glowing with evil. No-one knew what to do. Call the fucking RSPCA like there was a dangerous dog on the loose? Well he wasn't exactly behaving like a human being.

I started to have serious pains in my stomach and chest and was in and out of the hospital around that time. First, they discovered I had a gastric ulcer, caused by all of that drinking and stress. Second, they thought I had an inflammation of the heart, but in the end they decided I was suffering with severe anxiety, probably caused by watching my mates turn into dogs and hugging foxes. So I was quite unwell at that stage in my life.

I knew that ecstasy and cannabis were bad for me so I managed to quit, and quitting at that age was extremely hard with all the peer pressure and hanging around with the same mates who hadn't quit. This was when I realised I had strong willpower and the ability to fight back mentally. For example, I was always convinced I was going to die, my anxious thoughts were telling me this constantly. I would start feeling dizzy and get hot and cold sweats. 'I'm gonna die, I'm gonna die,' I would be thinking. But I fought back telling those thoughts, 'Go on then, kill me, I don't care if I die'. Simple but effective. How can you worry about dying when you don't give a toss whether you die or not? But don't get me wrong. Those thoughts and fears didn't stop there, but my little fight back helped no end.

I spent some days alone at my mother's home. These times were passed mostly by reading. While my other mates were out inhaling solvents, I was in W H Smith's stealing biographies. I would then escape from my disturbed life for a while reading about other people's adventures. I especially loved reading true crime books. I'm not one of those plastic people who wants a book out and on the shelf about my own hard times and life of crime, because what you are reading right now is just the thoughts of a twenty-four-year-old–and that's not a life. Most of these guys I read about were getting into their fifties by which time they were just about sorting themselves out. Their parents had passed away whilst those authors were in jail and their wives had had enough and cleared off with someone else. And anyone who wants that type of life is a complete mug. If you have tasted the prison system like I did you wouldn't want to go back, which I will come to later. But how can you just stop a criminal mind overnight. You can't. How else can you replace the buzz of getting away with a bag of money? Fuck me, I'm getting carried away. I was only fifteen remember, life was still good.

Steve's violence continued and became more unpredictable. One day he picked up a hoover in his front room and beat another boy senseless with it. The violence we all witnessed in that House of Horrors was brutal. Then Steve was spotted by a neighbour wielding the machete on the balcony and before you know it we had the riot police at the door complete with shields. Steve was made to leave the house in his boxer shorts with his hands on his head, so he couldn't conceal the weapon. I can understand why the police would use this procedure, but making a thirteen-year-old boy stand in his boxers for the world to see, that ain't right. The police then began to search us and the house, but they didn't seem to notice the little cupboard above the front room door. If they had opened it they would have found the machete, a Samurai sword and a whole arsenal of weapons.

I was beginning to wish I had never stolen that machete from Stitch's stash, that tool had a lot of blood on it. Steve would no doubt kill someone with it so I did the right thing and threw it away. Steve was heart-broken, to him it had become his life and protection, the tool of his trade. After Stitch found out the truth I'm sure he wasn't too bothered about not getting it back. Stitch was from Mitcham, but was a Morden WZ boy. He was always up for a drink and a bit of madness. It was time for another brew-raising adventure and remember I told you fights could take place with shopkeepers—well this time around there would be a couple of good 'uns. Me, Tony, Lend and good old Stitch were out on a brew-raise one evening. The nice thing about our gang was that whoever you bumped into on the streets you would meet up with WZ boys and girls and a party would start. The drinks were already flowing that night but we needed more, so the four of us headed-off on the bus to Cheam. With my big boom box blaring we were on a high, we headed into the first off-licence we saw, already so pissed-up that the shopkeeper was on alert and called for assistance. We were so drunk that we were openly stealing. As I left the shop, I was grabbed by a member of staff and a fight broke out. He ripped the hood off of my jacket and flung me onto the floor. I was lying there kicking out when all of a sudden the shopkeeper picked up the National Lottery sign and began to beat me with it. Tony came steaming in and began to smash my boom box over the shopkeeper's head, but the music stopped as the boom box smashed into pieces and the batteries fell out following which Tony started launching heavy duty batteries at the shopkeeper's head. Things were kicking-off big time.

Stitch was fighting in the shop and Lend was helping him to get out. We managed to regroup and ran a short distance before we stopped. We were in hysterics. It never occurred to us that the police were on their way and we casually walked down the road for ten minutes until we came to one of our favourite brew-raising shops. The plan was to steal more alcohol and some cigarettes. We sleeved our brew, then I ordered forty Benson and Hedges. When the shop worker put them on the counter, Tony grabbed them and we ran for the door. The shopkeeper managed to grab Stitch, who reached out for a bottle of red wine and smashed it clean over the shop workers head—you couldn't tell what was blood and what was wine. Stitch then ran for it. As we made our getaway through some wasteland we lit our cigarettes, unaware that half of the Sutton police force was out looking for us.

The next stop was the twenty-four hour Tesco store. We walked in and headed straight for the beer section, then as we made our exit a game of football started with a water melon. Unaware the security guard was on our tail, we headed over to the Tesco garage across the carpark. As me, Tony and Stitch messed about I turned and saw Lend lying on the floor. He was on top of the security guard and being held in a head lock. What a funny sight I thought and I noticed the look on that security guy's face when he realised he was losing the battle. I couldn't stop laughing at him and he just stared back in fear.

Stitch then found a fire extinguisher. He approached the guard on the floor and sprayed him in the face. The extinguisher sprayed out white powder and before you knew it the whole garage forecourt was one massive white cloud. What a sight I must say! Lend broke free and we all legged it. The guard couldn't see which direction we ran in, it was so cloudy. We walked about ten minutes through a couple of roads when all of a sudden police seemed to arrive from everywhere. There was nowhere to run this time and an officer pulled out my hood which had been found at the first scene. It matched my jacket and I was nicked. We were charged with a number of offences such as section 18 grievous bodily harm, actual bodily harm, robbery and criminal damage. We were so drunk and reckless we were totally oblivious to the trail of destruction we had left behind.

In the end the police decided to take no further action. Tony was charged with stealing cigarettes and Stitch with GBH for bottling the shopkeeper. For us lads this was close on being an average night out and all but forgotten about within a week because some other dramatic incident would have taken place. Stitch was fifteen at the time of these offences. A year later he would face a much more serious charge.

One night a small group of Morden WZ boys decided to go on a fishing trip to Hampton Court—a nice break from the madness of Morden. With a few beers and a couple of spliffs they laughed and joked looking like normal teens. Some local girls walked by and a few jokes between the groups soon turned into an argument, but nothing unusual by WZ standards. The girls made threats and then left. Around fifteen minutes later Stitch and the others were alerted to an older boy approaching who was drunk, shouting abuse and armed with a wing mirror as a weapon. Stitch was using crutches at the time so was definitely the weaker of the two. The older boy approached and started to hit Stitch with the wing mirror. He turned out to be the boyfriend of one of the girls who had walked past earlier. Stitch, in a loosing battle, reached for a fishing knife and that split second decision changed both their lives. Stitch stabbed the boy once, but once was enough to kill. The knife blade penetrated the boy's heart and he fell to the ground.

I was later told by a WZ boy who witnessed the incident that the victim lay on the floor having a fit before he passed away. Stitch and the others ran and in true WZ fashion headed for the railway tracks and made their getaway. News got back about how the boy had died and now Stitch was wanted for murder. He was convinced by somebody's father to hand himself in and that's what he did. I believe that in the circumstances Stitch should have been convicted of manslaughter, but he was convicted at the Old Bailey of murder. He received a sentence of detention for life at Her Majesty's pleasure—at the age of just sixteen. One tragic response and he was banged up for life.

At the time of writing this, Stitch has been in prison for around seven years. Later, whilst serving a short prison sentence in Feltham Young Offender Institution I was released on Christmas Eve and as I left in the morning to head to the gate on my way out I saw him looking through the bars at me. He shouted out for me to write to him. I was heading home for Christmas and he was staring at a lifetime in prison. That hurt me. I can't say I felt his pain, but I felt bad on his behalf. It upsets me today thinking of him just sitting in his cell with no release date. Yeah he took a life, but it was far from a cold-blooded killing. I've heard of cases where a victim has been stabbed five times but where the offender was only convicted of manslaughter. I appreciate that a teenager died that day and a family was left broken, but the judge himself hit home when he referred in court to, 'A fateful night when two young men lost their lives'.

But let's get back to the demonic days of Crazy Steve and his little House of Horrors. On Steve's fourteenth birthday his father, Brendan, bought him some cannabis, just one example of Steve's unstable upbringing. But now Brendan was gone, Steve ran the house. Within months the state of it had deteriorated, and nearly all of the walls were covered in demonic drawings and splatterings of blood. It was not a healthy environment even for the most veteran of squatters and there you had a group of teenagers living in pure squalor. We would sit around at three in the morning and wait for lone men to walk past the house. Suddenly we would spot one. We would then cover our faces with anything we could find such as bin bags or tea towels, then we would hunt our victim down and rob him. Those crimes were utterly disgusting and disgraceful, we were like a pack of feral animals hunting our prey, causing our victim's years of trauma, all for a few measly quid.

Those actions were bad but Crazy Steve had a more brutal blood lust than the rest of us put together. Whilst he was still in possession of his cherished machete he would go out and rob people late at night on his own. I remember him taking me to the location of one attack he had carried out on a man. To this day I'm not sure if he used the machete or not. When I got there I saw a pool of blood covered by sawdust.

Steve would wrap up a brick in a sweatshirt and beat his victim with it. He once told me his favourite part of an attack was when he saw the look of terror in his victim's eyes as he drank their blood. At the age of fifteen I had witnessed a lot of violence, but Crazy Steve was on another planet and I was scared stiff of him. I would have sleepless nights when I saw visions moving around my room and believed that they were demons coming to get me. Christians use the term 'smothering' and this is what I experienced on a number of occasions, especially around the days of Crazy Steve. Being smothered meant that I would wake-up in the middle of the night lying flat on my back. My eyes would be wide open but my body would be held to the floor by some kind of spiritual force. I would be screaming out for help, for my mum, but no words would be coming from my mouth. This was my state of my mind back then. I would be completely terrified. I would have the most disturbed nightmares and remember them clearly the following day.

One of the scariest of these was of being in my old house in Carshalton. I would be sitting in the front room, the walls dripping with blood and grime, the front windows wide open with the curtains blowing outwards in the wind. I would walk to the window and look out and see a hill. The night was dark and cold and all around me was a graveyard. Then I would be stuck in this cemetery running for my life, being chased around the hill and falling over gravestones, unable to escape. Just as I was about to die I would wake up in terror, sweating and petrified.

Without it being spoken about, Steve became my master when it came to the demonic stuff and even though I was scared stiff I would still want to impress him. Even though Steve thought a lot of me I was still very wary of him. Whilst sitting talking to him in his bedroom one day I saw his crazy smile freeze, then his bedroom walls which were battered by multi-coloured graffiti started to bleed black and red. I sat there in horror as they seemed to run with blood. Steve just sat there frozen, smiling.

Another time whilst sitting in his room I noticed around twenty green stones sitting on a cabinet. I poked them with my fingers in curiosity when to my horror I realised they were stones from a grave. I sat there thinking, 'Fuck me, Steve is nuts'. I realised they were in the shape of a pentagram. A lot of Satanists use this as a symbol of evil. This demonic shit really fucked with our heads, really messed up our lives. Steve loved it but the rest of us remained scared stiff even if we held it all in.

I know for a fact this all had an impact on my mind. It caused me to have serious panic attacks, I was suffering from depression and I was self-harming regularly. With Brendan now in a rehab it wasn't long before social services caught on about Steve living on his own and with all of the disturbances caused by us in and around the House of Horrors it wasn't long before the council evicted him—and the rest of us. Steve was put in a children's home in north-London. So the Devil packed his bags, left the House of Horrors and went back to Hell. Yeah, I wish it was that easy, but the reality was we were all scarred by the demonic days and the Devil wasn't finished with us yet.

CHAPTER 8

WARRIORZ COME OUT TO PLAY

When Crazy Steve's house was no longer available we hung out on the Morden streets far more. Our base was now back at Sainsbury's car park. The whole place and surrounding alleyways were smeared with graffiti. Wimbledon police were not stupid. We were all well-known to them, and they realised that we were trouble. So they installed a dozen or so CCTV cameras around Morden. We knew where every one of them was positioned. There happened to be one right above a set of stairs where we used to congregate. The cameras would pick up on us, follow us through the town and eventually round the back to the stairs where that particular camera would stare at us constantly. The operator must have known each of us intimately and I guess by name. We would stick two fingers up and the camera would turn itself from side-to-side as if it was shaking its head at our antics.

Wimbledon police had had just about enough of the graffiti and seeing thirty drunken kids terrorising the community. It was time for them to get rough with us. Two riot vans filled to bursting with police officers would now circle Morden town centre day and night looking for us. If they saw us we were roughed up and provoked to get a reaction. If we reacted we were nicked. I guess they hated us and would rather see us all locked up and out of sight. They commented about us on a number of occasions in the local newspapers misdescribing us as 'Ward Zone'. We were the Warriorz mate, but still happy to be getting the publicity.

Whilst on a bus near Morden we spotted the riot van driving alongside and someone decided to spit out of the window at them. The blue lights went on and the police steamed the bus. Everyone sitting on the side of the bus which the spit came from was nicked, and once again I was lucky to have just moved seats. I got off and watched the police put Tony and Crazy Steve in the riot van which drove on a short distance where I caught up with it on foot. I looked in and saw my mates getting a kicking by the police. One officer had the peak of his cap wedged down into Tony's mouth. I couldn't help my friends, but that wasn't the first or last time I witnessed police brutality. What can what anybody do in such a situation? The police are a big army and they stick together. You will get to hear of an incident later on about how I was treated by Sutton police. That incident along with things that happened earlier during this particular night left me needing therapy.

The police won their little battle for now and we moved out of Morden until the heat died down. Our new location was Rose Hill, for all of WZ plus the local kids who came to join our gang. At our new spot, the drinking got out of hand. We progressed from drinking Stella to Tennants Super and from Tennants Super to whisky and were soon fully-fledged alcoholics. The thing about being a first-class drunk is that you seem to suffer from loss of memory. So I would wake–up in the morning having forgotten about a serious incident that took place the night before. My drinking was so bad it wouldn't be rare to see me sleeping on the street in broad daylight. I was really bad when I was under the influence of alcohol and I wouldn't think twice about using a weapon during a casual argument. I once bottled a local boy with three different bottles in one night. His name was Lloyd Lilley and he was much younger and smaller than I was. We kept bumping into each other that night and fighting and I was embarrassed because he was getting the better of me, so I bottled him every time I ran across him. After this we became friends and gained a mutual respect for each other. Years later I was looking out of my cell window one day and saw Lloyd and called out to him and we talked about the manor and so on. In late 2008 he was murdered. He was stabbed and had part of his ear cut off. The funeral was a truly sad occasion, just seeing the grief in his brothers' eyes affected me deeply.

Me and a friend did a special piece of graffiti dedicated to Lloyd in his back garden for his mother. Initially I didn't want to do it at first as I was awash with guilt because of the trouble the two of us had had going back. But another friend of mine who was one of Lloyd's best mates convinced me that I should. The whole manor was talking of Lloyd's death, so I know he will always be remembered. His death didn't surprise me, not because it was him but because as you grow up and leave youthful gangs and start getting into heavier things people start to lose lives — the next chapter in a young person's life when it becomes life or death on the destructive path of crime.

By now all of the local youth offending team believed that I was on the path to a life of crime. I was a persistent young offender, I drank, shoplifted, sprayed graffiti all over London, robbed people and was extremely violent. I even started to sell ecstasy for an older graffiti-writer called Sicko from the Croydon area. Sicko believed I would be good at it as I was respected around my local streets, but I was way too reckless and would have to go out and steal money to pay him back. So I got out of that game pretty sharpish. Sicko didn't get out of it alive. He moved up to selling harder drugs. One evening he left Croydon to head to Sutton, which was then rife with crack and heroin addicts. Waiting in an alleyway to make a deal with two drug-fiends who were in a state of agitation, they pulled a knife to rob him and ended up stabbing him to death. He lay there dying just because he wanted to turn a quick profit. His murder didn't even make the news and to the police it was just another black drug dealer off the streets and their books.

I wasn't too friendly with Sicko at the time of his murder. One day I went to Croydon to sell one of his friends a camcorder which I had stolen. I was getting around three hundred pounds for it. But what a mug I was passing through a different territory wearing a five hundred pound gold chain and a pair of Gucci sunglasses. I went into Kentucky Fried Chicken to meet Sicko's friend, headed for the toilet and was CS-gassed and robbed. I was down about a grand and a half's worth of goods but when I pleaded for Sicko's help he turned his back on me. The best thing I got out of that situation was that I learnt the lesson that I should only do business with my own and trusted people. If something is dodgy it is better to forget it. Also that what comes around goes around because nearly all of the goods I stole or had bought with dirty money, so how could I really complain?

A few weeks into our time in Rose Hill the place seemed to deteriorate, graffiti was sprayed-up everywhere, late at night shop windows got smashed. We were a complete nightmare for the local authority and the madness we created always seemed to follow us about. As a crazy boy you attract crazy girls and I had plenty of them. Enter Danielle, who was as mad as I was. She was always drunk and causing trouble, and for some reason we seemed to connect. I was now sixteen and like all the other boys in the gang was sexually active. Good old Danielle was sexually active with nearly all of us. She was so abusive and messed up that she loved me one minute and the next she would turn on me calling me a 'Paki' and throwing other insults. They were good times though. Like me, Danielle was from a mixed race (black and white) background. She lived with her mother and her step-dad. He was a right nutcase, and also a hardcore skinhead and racist, and he only tolerated Danielle because of her mum. Nowadays as a wiser young man I can look back and see why certain people were so messed up in their childhoods and as with me there was a method to Danielle's madness. Our on-off relationship evolved around getting pissed out of our heads and being abusive to each other—but, come on, it weren't that bad because one day I stole her a bunch of flowers from outside a shop! See, I am a bit of an old romantic, and being in love in your teens is the best. I should have given her a bunch of stinging nettles because all she gave me for the next couple of months was worry and stress. Let me explain.

Danielle phoned me one day and informed me she was pregnant, yeah and that the baby was mine. Fuck me I thought, my initial thoughts being that it wasn't. Well the word was she had gone through most of WZ and probably half of WK as well. But the phone calls didn't stop. If it wasn't her telling me the baby was mine then her mate would be phoning me to say the same thing even if I might have been taking a leaf out of my father's book and running away from my kid–if it was mine that is. The phone started to ring again and this time it was her step dad.

'Listen you little shit you got my Danielle pregnant.'

The levels of fear and stress I went through because of her and her family and the thought of becoming a father whilst I was so young meant that I was shitting myself. So I did what I was best at and that was knocking back some of grandpa's old cough medicine. Consumed by alcohol I drowned out the problems of my young life, even if when I woke in the morning the baby drama was still there.

Danielle came to meet me one day and she had been to have a scan. She showed me the picture and now it dawned on me that I *was* going to be a dad. My crazy state of mind seemed to calm down for a while. I was more relaxed, I felt like a man. I was pulled up by police in Balham and in my possession I had a brand new stolen phone in a box. They ran a name check and heard my previous over the radio and started asking questions about the phone. As

I talked to them I told them the phone was mine and I was going straight 'cos I was going to become a dad. I even showed them the scan photo. They could have nicked me for handling stolen goods but I got a pat on the back for being an expectant father and was sent on my way.

It was now coming-up to the next scan appointment. I went there along with Danielle and her mum. After talking to the nurse and working out the date when she got pregnant, that horrible feeling came over me of being used and cheated. The lying bitch, there was no way that baby could have been mine as I never slept with her around that time. I walked out of that hospital fucking broken and distressed from all that grief. I walked all the way home thinking who could I tell of my pain. No-one. I was fuming. I found out the original scan picture was of Danielle's younger sister's baby and I'm sure I never got her pregnant! I made my way to the fridge and found a bottle of my mum's wine. I sat in my bedroom and drowned my sorrows. Come five o'clock I was looking out of my bedroom window and noticed Danielle and her mum pull up outside. Well at least they were coming around to apologise I thought—but hold on a minute why were they going to my mate's house next door? Then I realised the baby belonged to him. She had literally been shagging the whole neighbourhood.

I once wrote down this whole incident in a long poem. I remember two lines of it went something like this:

'So I was never there with her in labour,
Found out the baby belonged to my next door neighbour'.

Once Danielle realised one hundred per cent that it wasn't mine she decided to have an abortion. I never did get an apology from here or her family, and after arguing with her one evening in Wallington her step dad and his skinhead mates turned up and started to chase me–and believe me they weren't shouting out, 'Please stop mate, we only want to say sorry'. But listen, that little episode with Danielle was kids stuff compared to the next episode. So tune in folks to 'Danielle and the Warriorz'. Coming-up next, a WZ boy will be receiving a life sentence.

I seemed to hit the bottle big time. Me, Joe and Tony drank anything that was put in front of us. Out on a brew-raising expedition it didn't take long to find what I was looking for and with a big bottle of Jack Daniels up my sleeve I was on my way. A disturbed sixteen-year-old with a big bottle of Jack Daniels at the ready equalled only one thing—it was a recipe for disaster. As I travelled back towards the new base at Rose Hill, I swigged constantly from that bottle. It wasn't long before I was on another planet altogether, even by my young wino standards I was gone. As I swaggered around Rose Hill talking to myself and shouting abuse at my shadow, my buzz was interrupted by two local bobbies who knew who I was. I was too drunk to realise what I was saying or doing, but a fair cop as they say, told me that if I left the area I would not get nicked for being drunk and disorderly, so I left. Fifteen minutes later I was back again arguing with me, myself and my shadow. This drew the attention of the same two police officers as before.

'Right you're nicked for being legless.'

Well I wasn't that legless because I broke from their grip and legged-it. I ran over to the local park and escaped from the clutches of the law. But in true 706-style I was back in Rose Hill within minutes, and this time the police nicked me good and proper. I was handcuffed and in their custody, well that's what they thought. They walked me over to their police car and stuffed me in the back seat. They then sat themselves down in the front seats and prepared to drive away. But at that moment half of WZ walked around the corner and crowded around the police car, screaming at them to let me go. People were kicking the car, spitting on it and rocking the car from side-to-side. All the while I was swaying backwards and forward on the back seat, not really knowing what was happening.

The police had no option but to get out of their vehicle and draw their truncheons. Pushing my fellow Warriorz up the street away from the front of the police car, the officers now had their backs to the police car. Two WZ girls opened the police car door and pulled me free. Handcuffed behind my back, I hid around the side of a bus stop. With my fellow Warriorz well aware of my being free–as they were facing the police car–they informed the police by screaming, 'Fuck, he's escaped'. The police turned around and to their horror saw an empty car with the passenger door wide open. Using a tactic usually used for stealing from shops my fellow WZ members distracted the police by saying that I had run the other way up an alley. Both the Warrorz and the police then set off up the alley 'chasing me', my team knowing that they were leading a false trail as I was heading in the opposite direction entirely. With two WZ girls either side of me, their arms around me, I was in Warrior heaven.

I hit every back alley and short cut to hide from the law as by now a search had begun. But it wasn't your usual game of catch a criminal. Sutton police were now trying to save their own skin. How do two police officers lose a vulnerable, paralytic, handcuffed sixteen-year-old, and how could he just disappear from the back of a police car? What if their charge fell down in a ditch and died alone in his handcuffs? There could well have been repercussions if I had come to any harm, so they pulled out every last stop to find me. There were police cars circling the area, police stationed outside my mother's house, search teams, the dog section and last but not least the copper chopper hovering above. Even with all this they still couldn't find me. I knew that whole manor like the back of my hand plus I had two fit Warrior birds with their arms around me covering the handcuffs. I managed to find my way back to a house in the Sutton area, and after several attempts by the girls to cut the handcuffs off failed I fell into a deep sleep with my hands turning blue. When I awoke I wasn't much more sober or in contact with reality, but it was time to hand myself in. The party was over. I could have been found dead in a ditch, but I wasn't ready to die. I still had a lot of madness to get through before that.

As I walked towards the police station I was wrestled to the ground by a group of officers. I was under arrest for being drunk and disorderly, escaping from police custody and, get this, criminal damage to the handcuffs! I doubt a magician would have been able to saw them off whilst they were on his wrists and behind his back. But maybe I was turning into a magician. Abracadabra and I was out of that police car.

The officers that had lost me were not too happy with me following my arrest, and after that they were on my case every time they saw me drunk or not, but for some strange reason they always decided not to arrest me. I got proper respect for that episode, craved madness in my life and was infamous for being a nutter in at least five different boroughs. But being a nutter, a nut job, a madman, call it what you will was a lonely life. A wise man once told me, 'Don't you take the role of a madman in your gang. You will end up sad and lonely when they're all gone'. Those words were a painful truth. I was a lost boy and only heading in one direction–death or jail.

To me at the age of sixteen, seeing someone get stabbed, or beaten up was now normal. I was immune to hardcore brutality. I was self-harming in other crazy ways instead of just cutting my arms. I would punch my fists through windows to feel the pain and see the blood. One of my not so good nights I started to run head first into a shop shutter. I just couldn't stop myself. I ran at it about five times and believe me the pain was bad. But I hated my fucking life and hated myself and I wanted to feel pain. On the sixth go I ran at the shutter with so much force that, after my head hit it, I rebounded off it and flew in mid-air backwards, landing on the ground. I was unconscious for about ten minutes. Someone who knew me saw what had happened, took their coat off and put it under my head for comfort. That's what I needed, a bit of comforting, a shoulder to cry on, but for the moment I was sparko.

I woke and could feel blood pissing from my forehead. The wound was the shape of a triangle, but the piece of cut flesh pointed upwards which made it look diamond shaped. I felt an awful pain in my head. I looked into the mirror and saw the diamond on my forehead. Without thinking I decided that I would cut off the loose skin to make it look better. I got a pair of scissors and lined them up with the triangle shaped piece of dry skin and snipped.

'Aaaaaaaaaah,' the skin *wasn't* dead after all, it was all too alive and I had just cut it through with a pair of scissors. I've never felt pain like that before and the sheer shock and agony nearly knocked me back out again. My days as a plastic surgeon were over. And because of my handiwork I have a lump of dead skin on my forehead for life that looks like the biggest zit you've ever seen. As Sirus the leader of the gang in the New York-based classic film 'The Warriors' declared, 'One gang could run this city'.

'Can you dig it?'

'Yeah.'

'Can you dig it?'

'Yeah.'

'Can you dig it?'

'Er, no mate.'

I don't know whose bright idea it was, but someone somewhere thought it would be a good idea to call a truce between WZ and WK. The police were well aware of our ongoing feud. My stepdad Gary who worked for British Telecom was once installing new telephone lines at Kingston Police Station when he looked up and saw a photo of good old me with my fellow Warriorz. The police though weren't too bothered about a truce, they wanted us all nicked. From day one of this talk I was not the slightest bit interested. First-off we were Warriorz not the Peacemakers. It wasn't just a name, it was our whole being–and Warriorz don't call truces for nothing. Secondly the proposed gang was to be called WKZ, for 'Warrior Kingz'. Other names were suggested, but for me it was still the same issue, and my answer was a big fat no to any talk of a ceasefire!

Originally, our war was over the fact that our gang names sounded so similar, so why should our gang be called WKZ, why should there be a K before the Z? In any event, WK didn't like me and I could never feel one hundred per cent safe in their territory. I was hurt by the fact that my fellow Warriorz wanted to join forces and even though I disagreed they went ahead with it. So I always stayed behind when both gangs met. My friend Joe, cousin Tony and all of the others went along for the ride. Me and Crazy Steve stayed in our manor and were fuming at them for their disloyalty. You can imagine the chaos there would be with both gangs standing side-by-side. I heard the story of how fifty of them would steam shops for alcohol and one newspaper wrote that a store manager quit after WKZ turned up saying, 'How can I possibly work in a shop when fifty rowdy kids turn up and turn the place over'. He threw in the towel after that. It wasn't just the thieving of alcohol, it was the drinking and fighting that went with it. What other gang in south-west-London would want to stand up to both gangs in combination and ready to fight tooth and nail as one unit. The only other 'gang' was the police and on the night in question they were outnumbered heavily.

There was talk of a massive party at a pavilion in Potters Park just behind the St Helier estate. With WKZ hovering around the nearby towns knocking back drink after drink, it wasn't long before they wanted to have a little boogie on the dance floor. They entered the pitch black park and all fifty of them started to make their way to the gates of the party. It wasn't long before the three burly bouncers noticed an army marching towards the gate. As quick as they could they swung the gates closed and locked them even quicker. WZ and WK didn't go there to wait in the cold, so the night kicked off with a bottle getting thrown, next a brick or two until people started to pull on the gates. The veteran bouncers were now shitting it. It didn't take long for fifty drunk, hardened and rowdy kids to rip the whole gate off and start bringing the walls down and it soon turned from wanting to boogie to rioting. WKZ steamed the party and those big bouncers had fifteen and sixteen-year-olds trying to gouge their eyes out, confiscate the stock and the till and knock the DJ clean out. For fifteen minutes WKZ ran that party and believe me they had a blinding time.

It wasn't long before the law turned up to spoil the show. I don't think they realised the scale of what was happening. Two carloads of coppers got out and tried to calm things down. Fuck me, even Ghandi couldn't calm down WKZ. In no time at all the police officers were surrounded and they were beaten all over that park. The wounded officers sounded a Code Red, which means every available police car or van must rush to their assistance straightaway. Well the bastards would be needing a lift home. I can't name names but my mate climbed on top of the car and started to kick the blue lights in, and when that failed he ripped them clean off with his bare hands letting out an almighty roar as he did so as they smashed down on the ground. Now with a WZ boy wearing a policeman's hat and jumping up and down on top of the car this was a proper party. Both police cars were left looking like they had been in a serious collision. All you could hear for miles was the sound of sirens. It was time for my fellow Warriorz and WK enemies to make a quick exit. Most of the mob got away through the parks in the darkness, but some were arrested and severely dealt with. That night both gangs stamped their reputations on south-London writing gang folklore as two groups of kids jointly took street life to the next level. Shame I wasn't there, but as I said WKZ wasn't for me.

Joe and Nemz told me that they were meeting with the two top WK boys. I was invited but said I would phone them back and let them know. But of course I had other plans. I went to meet Crazy Steve and let him into my intention to disrupt things. Two top WK members on our manor, this was to good to be true. The plan was for me to arrange to meet Joe, Nemz and the two WK members like I was coming in peace, but I was a Warrior and you must know what that meant. Me and Crazy Steve popped a bottle of vodka and in no time at all were geared up to cause trouble so as to put an end to this WKZ shit. There was already by now an unwritten rule that gang members were safe in the territory of each other, so the two WK members arrived at the meeting spot without concern. They saw me coming and it was all smiles and handshakes until Joe and Nemz saw Crazy Steve march around the corner. Without hesitation he attacked the WK boys. They must have thought Joe and Nemz had set them up, and the truce was now well and truly over. The two WK boys ran off screaming revenge, whilst Joe and Nemz were shouting at me and Steve.

We replied like a bunch of hyenas, grunting and laughing and jumping about. We were overwhelmed with joy at the fact that we had taken these guys out and ruined the proposed alliance. I was now so drunk I walked off and left my friends. I sat on the floor outside Morden Station, then decided to lie down on the floor and fell asleep in broad daylight to wake up surrounded by concerned members of the public.

'Don't be concerned. This is my disturbed young life. It happens.'

With that thought in my head I decided to leg it before the police turned up.

I was sixteen, beyond help and things were only going to get worse, but I loved the pain of those streets. I didn't think much of myself. But it was a case of bring it on, bring the craziness to me, it was my life, who I was in those days. And with that the madness kept on coming.

CHAPTER 9

WHEN MORDEN BECAME A WAR ZONE

Now around this time I did try to do a college course or two but they didn't
come to much. Even though I wasn't close to my mum, as she worked at
Carshalton College she would try to get me on courses. The thing is with my
anxiety so bad I just couldn't hack it. I would sit in a new class for five minutes, panic, be overwhelmed, walk out and start running away—and then
feel utter relief for having escaped. I would run as fast as I could and think to
myself, 'I'm fucking mental, no one is even chasing me'. People would say,
'Why don't you try this or that training course'—but I never had any ambi-
tions in the direction of work. The longest I ever stayed any distance at all with
one was when I attended one on painting and decorating for five weeks but
in the end got kicked off for bei [handwritten: Anxiety-prevents Justin from settling into]
me to attend for that long, and [handwritten: courses/new environment]
I had turned over a new leaf. [handwritten: - loss of control of the situation.]
[handwritten: - loss of power / authority]
    With these courses not worl
builder she knew. I waited at tl
up, jumped in and gave the guy a nod. There was a deathly silence the whole
fifteen minute journey to the site.'

    This guy thinks I'm a weirdo,' I thought.

    When we arrived he gave me a pair of gloves and a tool and told me to
scrape up some hard bits of cement on the floor. Once again panic hit.

    'I'm doing a shit job, he's watching me,' I thought, 'fuck this, I have to
escape.'

    But what could I do? I was in full panic attack mode and thinking, 'Shall
I beat him over the head with this tool?' I quickly dismissed that thought,
but when he went around the side of the garage I quietly put the tool down,
slipped off the gloves, tiptoed out of the garden and ran. As I sprinted off
I felt on top of the world, no more anxiety. I was straight on the bus, back

to Morden and safety. But come on, you must be able to understand that I had quite a few problems in my life and was finding it hard interacting with normal people. I was more used to associating with Devil worshippers, raving alcoholics and desperate street kids. The builder later told my mum that he had turned around to find me gone—and wondered what had he done wrong. I thought, 'Sorry mate, it just ain't working out between us, I like to cut my arms and you like to build houses'. It was like Forest Gump, but I never had Jenny to guide me, I had Danielle shouting out, 'Run Sevens run'.

I may have a laugh and joke while I am writing this but I was an unhappy, sad kid. I never knew what normality was. I used to run away from all kinds of things, but I could never escape from myself and my own self-destructive urges and thinking. I was drunk most of the time, to the extent of pouring Tennants Super in my cornflakes. By now I was also beginning to show some real symptoms of mental illness, as if I haven't described enough of them already. One evening whilst walking to Rose Hill with a bottle of whisky in my hand I started to feel really ill. It was as if I was going to drop down dead there and then. I walked to the local hospital and mumbled to the receptionist that I was dying and needed help.

'Alright love, just sit and wait there,' she replied.

I sat down for five minutes by which time I had had enough of waiting so I pretended to collapse on the floor. I lay there for a minute until some nurses rushed out to help me. They put me in a wheelchair and pushed me through to the children's accident and emergency department. A right result, no two hour wait for me and I didn't even have to walk, being wheeled there by nice nurses. As I lay on the hospital bed I started to become more and more irritated. I managed to steal a pair of scissors and began to cut my arms. My mum was called to the hospital and couldn't believe the state I was in. I then entered psychotic mode screaming the Devil this and the Devil that. It reminds me of that scene in 'The Exorcist' where the girl is lying on her bed possessed. My mum had never seen me like this and I believe she was heartbroken due to just how crazy I was becoming. We weren't close but we loved each other even if we never said it. I knew I was hurting her, but was helpless at that point.

Due to my condition the nurses reached for the phone and called a psychiatrist from the Sutton mental health team. The woman doctor examined me physically and mentally, firing questions such as, 'Do you see demons? Do you worship Satan?' I was thinking,

'No you silly bitch, I just witnessed one of my friends messing around with the bloody dark arts and this had a serious affect on me and on my mates as well.'

I know that me, Tony and Joe were all affected by Crazy Steve's behaviour. We were the most widely known of our gang and were always respected because we were up for being rowdy. We bounced off of each other's rowdiness and half the time were a bad influence on each other. The other half of the time we were street brothers. We supported each other through the harshest of times. Me and Tony even cried together about our lives. Joe once hugged me and told me I was like his little brother. We kept each other warm mentally whilst sleeping rough on the streets. We wrote to each other when we were in prison. When Joe was in hospital with pneumonia I was the only one who visited him, because under the crazy barrier that had built up around me I also had a heart. I was polite around people's parents and my wider family.

The thing about Joe was that he would always end up in the wrong place at the wrong time. He wasn't one of the luckier ones and seemed to get caught for silly things and end up behind bars. He once fell out with a Morden girl and a big argument erupted, with the girl screaming that he had better watch his back. An hour later this big geezer turned up, punched him and gave Joe a massive black eye. Fuming, Joe decided to go and steal a couple of beers, entered the local Safeway's and was spotted sleeving. A wrestling match began between him and a big-built security guard and they both managed to squeeze out of the door still holding on to each other, but the security guard punched him in the other eye, leaving him with two black eyes.

See what I mean? He wasn't the luckiest. But he was a decent kid at heart who found himself trapped in this gang we'd created. Though I say 'trapped', I don't mean he or any of the rest of us always wanted to escape from it, but that this lifestyle had just became our reality. We were all feeling pain from things that were happening to us on the streets and in jail. But when you're a scared teenager who do you tell, where do you go for help? I can spot the young troubled kids these days from the way they act, or I sometimes overhear them talking about the things they get up to—and I sense it when they're in a downward spiral. It is the same way that me and my friends went, suffering from trauma, including from the violent situations we had witnessed.

I don't understand why judges or probation officers didn't offer us a bit of therapy, we witnessed more then a few beatings and we took beatings every other week. I believe that as young teenagers the system failed us. Kids need guidance, not locking up or being beaten up by the police. The more violence we witnessed the more violent our own lives became.

An argument can turn into a right bloody mess and I will give you an example. Me and Joe had what we classed as our own special reckless days. We would leave the others behind and just the two of us would go out brew-raising and getting up to mischief. These were the days when we were closest and the best of friends. I would get into a fight with a big man and as the man roughed me up and because I was only a little runt, Joe would jump in and defend me. During one of our crazy days it escalated into something bigger with five WZ boys ending up behind bars. Me and Joe were strolling through the back streets of Morden when we walked past an ex-girlfriend's house. We noticed her speaking to a couple of older Somalian boys. She was giving us wanker signs and evil stares. Me and Joe shouted abuse back and squared up to the Somalians. We swore revenge and ran around the corner to our friend Little Adam's house, knowing full well he had a collector's arsenal of weapons. We banged on the door and when he opened it we told him about our beef with the Somalians and asked to borrow some weaponry. He came back with a sword and a machete and passed them out to us.

It was a boiling hot day and people were out gardening and enjoying the sun. Me and Joe, now armed to the teeth, ran past the old folks weeding their gardens as they looked up in disbelief. We made it back to my ex-girlfriend's house and the two Somalian guys were still there, so we ran straight up to them, threatening them with our newly acquired weapons. Now *they* were shitting themselves. Who knows what we would had done to them if Little Adam's dad had not spotted us as he drove past. He jumped out of his car, took the weapons from us and was absolutely livid with us both.

Me, Joe and Little Adam left for another part of Morden and Joe then left us to go and meet some other members of WZ. An hour or so had passed since the earlier incident was all but forgotten when my 'phone rang and a WZ member alerted me to be on the lookout as there were now around thirty Somalians searching for us all over town. Me and Little Adam started to head towards the town centre via the back alleys. As we walked out of one of these to the main road, I told him to hold back whilst I checked whether the coast was clear. I poked my head out and took a look. Fuck me, I saw an army marching in my direction. I was certain they never spotted me and retreated saying, 'Fucking run, run man'.

We could have run straight on and out of the other side of the alley and to safety but the adrenalin was pumping. I took a left turn into a small alley-way behind the back of some shops leading to a dead end. We looked at each other hoping I had not been spotted then waited and waited. All of a sudden one of the Somalians walked past the entranceway to where we were hiding. In slow motion he turned and locked eyes with us. We were his prey. With a sick smile and happy at his find he summoned the other twenty-nine and pointed towards us. Having had a sword and a machete pulled on them earlier, they came equipped with metal poles and baseball bats. I looked at Little Adam and turned and ran towards the end of the passageway. With nowhere else to run I thought it was all over for the two of us. If I had not had a sharp eye we could have been savagely beaten. In a split second I noticed a door at the back of a shop which was open, and without hesitation ran inside. We were in the kitchen of a posh Italian restaurant. The chefs and dish-washers looked at us in shock as we ran through another door and entered the dining area. The gang of Somalians followed suit, waving their poles and bats in the air. As we ran through the packed dining area I noticed customers in shock at seeing us run past them and disappear out of the front door—and they nearly spat out their food and drinks when they saw the mob of Somalians chasing behind.

We were now running through the town centre. We didn't know it at the time but around ten WZ boys were across the road and watching in bemusement as they saw me and Little Adam and the Somalians in hot pursuit. Lady Luck must have had a fuck that day because she was on our side. Another ten WZ Stockwell boys had just jumped off of the tube in Morden and teamed up with those who were already there. They all came to our defence whilst we hid in Iceland. The Somalians were screaming for our blood at the front door, not realising that the WZ boys were heading across the road towards them.

Like I said about Joe, he was a bit unlucky at times. Oblivious to what was happening, he came strolling down the road and was spotted by the Somalians. They didn't waste time before attacking him. As this incident took place, our mob came charging in, and with that me and Little Adam ran out to join the rumble. There were scuffles and beatings going on everywhere. As I was punching a guy on the head I received a broken finger from one of my team who was bottling him but hit my hand by mistake as we struck at the same time. The geezers from the pubs came out to watch the battle and holding-up their pints cheered us on. I looked across the road and noticed one of the enemy lying on the cab office floor behind the front door. Tony was opening and shutting the door repeatedly with force, banging it on the guy's head. It was a scene of mayhem and the whole of Morden town centre came to a halt, panic alarms going off everywhere. Buses had stopped and traffic was at a standstill as we rioted in broad daylight. A car suddenly came swerving through the traffic and screeched to a halt. The doors swung open and Little Adam's brother-in-law and Crazy Steve appeared, bare-chested and wielding their own baseball bats. They steamed over and began to knock out the enemy. As this happened, a Somalian hit Adam around the head with a brick, knocking him unconscious. With that his brother-in-law picked him up and threw him into the back of the car as they and Crazy Steve quit the scene. It was mental and with no regard for the law.

We wasted the Somalians. They got absolutely slaughtered and in full view of the CCTV operators who no doubt watched on in disbelief. The police didn't dare enter the area until they had reinforcements but by now we knew it was time to run, so we all legged it and climbed into the tube depot to hide. We ducked down as we heard sirens in every direction. We knew we couldn't hide there for long and that we had to get out of the town, so the ten of us jumped back out of the tube depot and began to run to a bus stop. There, in the panic, we climbed aboard a single decker bus, but this particular bus was heading back through Morden. As it drew closer we could see the trail of destruction. There were police everywhere, uniformed officers and those in plain clothes. There were weapons such as bricks and metal bars scattered on the streets and we could see three Somalian boys slumped against the wall, covered in blood. As the bus passed this scene we tried to duck down but were spotted and three plainclothes policemen with walkie-talkies began chasing the bus.

We were screaming for the driver to put his foot down like the poor bloke was our getaway driver but with this he brought the bus to a standstill. The police boarded but didn't have a clue if we were the perpetrators or not. They didn't know which gang we belonged to, if any, and there seemed to be a lot of confusion between them. We all denied having been at the scene. They checked our hands for cuts and bruises then took our details and let us leave. Little Adam and a few other WZ boys went to hospital where they bumped into the wounded Somalians, and when security realised there was about to be another brawl they separated the two groups.

The 'phone rang at about seven in the morning. It was a WZ member warning me that Wimbledon police dressed in riot gear and carrying shields were raiding homes in connection with the riot. With that I left our house and stayed clear of it for a time. I later learned that five WZ boys got arrested for violent disorder, which is a charge one level below rioting. Two of them, the Terrible Twins, were arrested after the police scanned the CCTV footage but in the end they couldn't decide which of them it was who had been involved, so they were both released without charge. Being a lucky little shit, I had taken part in an attack that wasn't covered by the CCTV network, so I was still free and running wild.

Several of my friends were in the dock at Kingston Crown Court for this matter and went to prison for various periods of time. Other gangs kept coming to challenge us but we never lost in our beautiful town of Morden. It protected us with its rooftops and alleyways. Later on in life I became friends with the Somalian's 'top boy'. You sometimes make a good friend from an old enemy, after gaining mutual respect for each other.

Keith Gormley had just been released after serving a big stretch for his brutal bottle attack a few years back. His brother Kenneth still has time to do before he is released. Keith wanted to be with the new kids on the block and soon started knocking about with us. This was a recipe for disaster. He already had a reputation for being a bit of a nutter. But it seemed to be our destiny for him to be in our gang, we always welcomed trouble with open arms—and something was about to happen which would shock even our hardest members to the core. The Devil was back in town and was about to thoroughly enjoy himself.

CHAPTER 10

ONE TOO MANY PSYCHOPATHS

The first year of the New Millennium was nearly over and what a year it had been in our young lives. All the big talk of a computer meltdown never came true. Manchester United lifted the Premier League title for the sixth time, losing only three games in a whole season, but I don't think too much of that because I'm a Chelsea boy!

I'll try and tell you some more interesting facts about the year 2000. It had also seen me turn into a more disturbed and violent individual and it wouldn't be the last time I would be in that state. I had left my spell in Feltham Young Offender Institution behind, but the memory of it all came back to me when I saw on the news that a young Asian kid had been battered to death in his cell. Zahid Mubarek was someone with problems that had spiralled out of control. He was only serving a short sentence for minor offences. A lot of the youngsters in Feltham are vulnerable young boys who have had serious problems in their childhood. They then find themselves separated from their friends and families, locked up in a cell, scared and confused. Believe me, Feltham around the time was not a nice place to be. I was there and I saw with my own eyes kids being bullied and terrorised by the more hardened or older youths. With all of this going on and with the age of these boys I believe that such places have an enhanced duty of care over and above that involved in adult prisons such as Wandsworth Prison or Wormwood Scrubs.

In the early hours, whilst sleeping in his double cell, Zahid was savagely beaten to death with a table leg by his cell-mate Robert Stewart. The saddest things about it were that he was a known risk and Zahid was so close to being released, in literally a few hours time, following his last night in custody. Even after the inquiries and reports, serious questions still remain about how his death came about but that is something for another time and place.

My own experience of racism in Feltham relates not to other inmates but to that by prisons officers. During my first short but traumatic stay there from October to December 1999, I was racially abused by them. A good example is when me and a big black guy called Thomas worked serving-up the food together. Our nicknames, given by the officers, were Big Spoon and Little Spoon, rhyming slang for Big Coon and Little Coon. Officers would make remarks about the black and Asian kids, cursing them and making remarks like, 'Bloody niggers, fighting again' or 'Ahmed, clean-up your fucking cell, it stinks of curry'. Back then I would let out a nervous giggle if a screw racially abused me. I was too scared to say anything back. Later on in life I might have stabbed somebody for being racist towards me—and nowadays I would just laugh it off because I'm a happy, confident young man and the person who is coming out with the racist comments is the one who is bigoted, narrow-minded and insecure.

During the inquiry into Zahid's murder there was talk of officers setting up gladiator-style fights between prisoners of different races. Robert Stewart was known to have been involved in earlier violence, and staff at Feltham were, or should have been aware, of this. The establishment also had access to the racist letters that he was sending out to friends. I'm sure Mubarek's death could have been avoided. Around the same time there were a number of findings that the whole prison system and other parts of the system were affected by institutional racism and I know as a fact from my own experiences that no-one was standing-up for Asian and black kids. White kids were neglected daily in Feltham as well and the whole system stank. Even now, most of the kids in there have some kind of mental health problem or personality disorder. And believe me, due to my experiences there I certainly started to believe that some of the officers did!

Maybe the job itself attracts the odd psychotic individuals. When you hear the term 'psychopath' you naturally think of a machete-wielding, blood-hungry individual hell bent on killing someone. Sounds a bit like a few of my mob. But if you believe only that then you're wrong. I guess that there are undiagnosed psychopaths everywhere. The white collar psychopath is the one in the workplace, possibly your own boss or colleague. These types of individual might not hurt you physically but they can break you mentally, maybe by putting down your efforts and hard work or making other nasty comments which start to wear you down. They intimidate their fellow workers. They exhibit manipulative behaviour and demonstrate a lack of remorse. They may be glib and superficially charming, but they concentrate on leaving an indelible mark on their victims and on society. They may be cunning, self-centred, ruthless and terrifying, and they can make working life a living hell for many people. So what a thoughtful idea to give one of these psychopaths a job looking after youngsters, many of whom are quite vulnerable! There is also a risk of people like these finding their way into the police service, the army, schools, care homes for the elderly and anywhere else where they can get their kicks. So don't worry mum, I won't be sticking you in an old people's home when you go senile. You can come and live in a train depot with me!

You also get the odd pervert such as those who find nothing more satisfying than strip-searching young boys, Once whilst being strip-searched an officer gave me the once over as I was standing there naked, him the bastard in full uniform, looked towards my penis and exclaimed 'excellent'. I felt like grabbing the Biro from his table and shoving it through his eye.

So yes, poor Zahid Mubarek was set up to be attacked, or in a worst case scenario murdered. Following the uproar the case caused, the filthy system had a good scrub and let's hope that this will help to prevent something like it happening again—even if there is still a high level of deaths in custody generally. When Robert Stewart was sentenced, Mr Justice Grigson told him, 'As you are a danger to yourself and a danger to the public, custody for life is wholly appropriate.'

Returning to my survey of the year 2000, I was about to see one of my mob commit an act so violent that he too would be sentenced to life in prison. Me, Joe and the gang had done the odd bit of madness leading up to this point and we could've chosen to do something different and not gone on to do what we did. But fate is fate and like I said the Devil was out and about on those local streets.

As we walked towards a disturbance I noticed Danielle right in the thick of it—'Oh, here we go!' Danielle was also with a Warrior girl called Claudia. Well we all know what Danielle was like and this day she was having a slanging-match with three skinheads. We walked right into it. When she saw us approaching, she screamed at the three brutes, 'Watch now! ... My boys are here, just you watch!'. With that the skinheads attacked us. Joe was closest to them and was bottled by one of the men. In the midst of the screaming and shouting their three man army came steaming at us, tooled-up and screaming blue murder. With that we made our exit, but fifteen minutes down the road we regrouped. Joe, now with a big lump on his head and fuming that Danielle had got him into this mess. By this stage we were all well and truly tired, drunk and not making much sense at all. I looked down the road and spotted trouble on the horizon, from where Danielle and Claudia, a nice sort of girl who was just tagging along, were now marching towards us. As they got closer Joe and Danielle, who was shouting abuse at everyone, began a furious argument. She didn't apologise for getting Joe bottled but instead spat at him and threatened him. Then the pushing and shoving started and I got in between them to break it up. With me stuck in the middle, Danielle now carried on her verbal attack on Keith.

To calm the situation down, I convinced Danielle to come with me, which she finally agreed to do. So I left Tony, Joe, Keith and Claudia back at Rose Hill as me and Danielle walked on for about fifteen minutes. Even though she had tricked me with the pregnancy drama I still bothered to help her. As we sat on the wall of St Helier Hospital, we spoke about all sorts of things. It was now around three in the morning and there was nobody on the road. I looked into the distance and spotted a car heading in our direction, swerving about all over the place, the car horn waking-up everybody around. It came to a screeching halt in front of us. It was Danielle's mum, heavily intoxicated by alcohol and God knows what else. She screamed for me and Danielle to get into the car, as we were going to kill the boys who had terrorised her daughter. Hold on a minute, Danielle was the one who had terrorised my mates and I wasn't about to launch an attack on my own friends thank you very much. I had just got Danielle out of a mess and yet her mother wanted more trouble. Danielle jumped into the car and as I sat there on the hospital wall I watched it go, zig-zagging all the way up the road at speed in the direction of my other WZ friends. I sat there falling asleep. It had been a long day and it was about to turn into a long, horrific night.

Just as I was entering a deep sleep curled up on the wall, I was rudely awakened by my mobile 'phone ringing. It was Claudia.

'Quick, quick, run back to Rose Hill, something bad has happened.'

So with that I ran back there still half asleep, but I woke the fuck up with the scene I came across. Danielle was in hysterics, crying and screaming uncontrollably. I noticed that her mum was lying on the pavement with a blanket wrapped around her.

'He's stabbed my mum, help me ... he's stabbed my mum.'

Claudia explained that the car had pulled up close to her and my friends. Danielle and her mum had jumped from it and begun to attack Keith. You would have thought that with Keith stabbing a man earlier on in the evening that he would have had the common sense to get rid of the weapon. But Keith wasn't your normal Warrior, he was even more dangerous. When Danielle and her mum attacked he had reached for his knife and stabbed her mother in the stomach. Tony and Joe were as shocked as anyone that he could do such a thing. Even by WZ standards it was unthinkable. As kids we fought other kids and a few men, but to stab someone's mum, that was frightening and sickening.

My boys had run off by the time I arrived, Joe and Tony leaving the scene in shock and disbelief at the situation they had just found themselves in—and Keith running away from life in prison. I comforted Danielle as her mum was taken away in an ambulance. We then made the short walk to the hospital and as we sat in the family room to wait for news of her mum's condition I reassured her that everything was going to be fine. After waiting for an hour or so the doctors arrived and confirmed this. The knife had just missed her lung, but she needed an operation and had to be stitched-up internally.

Danielle's step-dad, the man who had terrorised me during Danielle's 'pregnancy' was screaming revenge on my friends. He was fine with me though for looking after Danielle. Me and Danielle then left the hospital knowing her mother was in a stable condition, and as we did so our eyes stung from the bright morning sky. Now almost sober and very tired, we headed for her house to catch some sleep, not knowing where my friends were by now. As I crashed out and for just a split second I felt that those twenty-four hours had been one long disturbed dream, but when I came round a few hours later I realised that the nightmare was a reality.

CHAPTER 11

RICH PICKINGS IN THE SMOKY CITY

How do you get over the fact that a member of your gang has just stabbed your ex-girlfriend's mum? I've always had a sixth sense for danger and could feel all day that there was violence in the air. I was sixteen-years-old with the world on my shoulders and a massive street reputation to protect, so there was no escaping the sickening dramas of that life. My self-destructive, life-threatening behaviour continued as Keith, Joe and Tony disappeared from the scene for a while.

Keith was wanted on suspicion of attempted murder initially, and Joe for allegedly punching Danielle, which was rubbish as it was only a reflex action because she was spitting in his face. Joe found himself caught up in this big case for pushing someone to stop himself being spat at and assaulted. Sutton police had thrown my name into the mix and the officer in charge of the case was trying to get a statement from me, or anybody else who was at the scene, even though I wasn't actually there at the time of the main crime.

Shortly afterwards, Keith and Joe were arrested. Keith was charged with grievous bodily harm with intent and Joe with punching Danielle. They were both remanded in custody. The officer in charge of the investigation somehow got my 'phone number and called asking for a statement about Joe assaulting Danielle. He also tried to scare me by saying I would be forced to go to court and stand in the witness box. I also found out that Danielle and her family wanted me to be a witness for the prosecution, in effect by asking me to lie and say Joe *had* punched Danielle first.

Well I politely told the officer to piss off. I would be at the court to defend my blood brother Joe. I would not be turning grass for anybody. Danielle was angry about what happened to her mum. That was understandable, but I wasn't about to let her stitch-up Joe. He was already sitting in a cell in Feltham for simply pushing her away. What happened between Keith and her mother was nothing to do with me and I wasn't helping anyone there, but I had a duty to help my innocent friend Joe. So I wrote to Joe and informed him not to worry as I'd be his witness at his trial, even if it did mean standing up in front of Danielle and her family and saying what really happened. He remained in custody waiting for his court appearance and we wrote to each other regularly.

What a start to the New Year hey, it was all happening. Already a 'middle-aged teen', I found a need for finer things in life such as clothes and girls. Always a good thief, I had started stealing when I was five-years-old. But back then I used to give all of the dodgy goods away to other kids. I once stole my teacher's gold parker pen as a gift for my mum after I had lost all connection with her due to her working all hours and sending me to Karen the child-minder way back. The sad fact is that is how I tried to win her back. I was trying to buy her love. This time around I'd be keeping the goods for myself. Some people say that there is no honour amongst thieves but I believe that hoary old line to be false—there can be a lot, but money changes people and, as the saying goes, it is the root of all evil. Let me demonstrate the economics of dirty money.

Two guys are potless so they decide to rob a brothel. One of them knocks on the door then enters when the working girl, Sarah, answers. He kicks up a bit of a fuss about the price he has to pay for personal services. This is all to see if a security guard comes to her aid. No-one appears, the man calms down and leaves quietly knowing now that he can easily return later with no fuss from a security guard. Then the two men wait until midnight to return, guessing that Sarah will have made a nice lump of money by then. The second man knocks on the door and Sarah believing he is an honest punter opens it, but suddenly the first man appears and the two of them burst in.

'Listen, bitch … just give us the money and you won't get hurt.'

She tries to put up a front that she's strong and won't hand over the money but eventually gives them 'half a bag of sand'. That five hundred pounds is very dirty money indeed, made from the vice game and it is now in the hands of two minor league robbers. Buzzing from their crime they head to their local boozer, laughing and showing their teeth like hyaenas. In good spirits, they flash their fast cash buying drinks for the ladies.

Soon, wanting to up the buzz, they phone a local foot soldier drug-dealer, who is a slave for the bigger dealer who sits on his arse counting his own dirty money with an evil grin. Foot soldier re-appears and is handed one hundred dirty vice-cum-robbery pounds. He replies by handing the robbers two weak wraps of cocaine. The hyaenas are happy with there prize and the foot soldier is happy that he can pay off some of his growing debt to his boss. The boss is only some wannabe gangster who thinks he is the dog's bollocks because he has a pound note or two. Not bothering about whether he he is fucking up peoples' lives by selling them drugs, instead he thinks he's the man, but he is surrounded by fake and evil people who are totally corrupted by the pound note — insecure, materialistic people who will walk the walk with you but sell their soul when a bigger fish arrives on the scene. Foot soldier now hands his boss one hundred pounds of dirty vice-cum-robbery-cum-drug money. Then it is back to work so he can pay off some of what he still owes.

Meantime the Big Bad Boss is getting ready for a night out in a local club, the place to be seen if you're a Big Time Charlie. The night is in full swing, champagne flowing, fake bird by his side, a few nods to the real gangsters in the club. He hands the barmaid one hundred pounds in twenty pound notes, now vice-cum-robber-cum-drug-cum-wannabe gangster money. He feels quite hard handing over that money knowing the tasty little blonde barmaid is on just six quid an hour. He gets his bottle of champagne and heads back off to his Dreamworld of gangsterism and respect.

The other man in the club is your average lad, out on the pull. Pissed out of his head he has no chance of pulling anything. So to help him boost his confidence he thinks it is a good idea to buy more drink, so he goes up to the blonde barmaid and hands her a fifty pound note. With a shit chat up line the girl quickly gives him his change which which includes two twenty pound notes of dirty money which originally came from the wannabe gangster's pocket. Your average lad drinks his drink and leaves with only one thing on his intoxicated brain. He desperately wants to get laid and so heads for the local brothel. After waiting for a time the door opens and standing there is, you guessed it, Sarah. There you have a cycle of dirty money. Can you guess which one I was in that tale. I was the security guard that didn't turn up for work!

To be honest, I hadn't worked much at all at that time because of the state of my mental health, but I was once a security guard in a brothel. My duties were to open the door to the punters and make sure they didn't rob the place. I also had to make sure the working girls were not mistreated by the punters.

If they became aggressive I would have to deal with the situation assertively, so I also had a club hammer as back up. I'm not trying to make myself out to be some sort of hard nut, but I had a duty to protect those women and their dirty money, so if you or anyone else had tried to take a liberty I would have got my hammer out. I was only getting paid fifty quid a night and after someone tried to rob the place and my hammer got pulled I realised it wasn't worth going down for manslaughter for that measly amount. For a few weeks until then I had begun to think that I was a working-class citizen not a hammer-wielding maniac. I couldn't continue if the working girls were more scared of me than they were of the robbers.

So other sources of dirty money caught my eye. As a street thief I would steal 'phones and electrical equipment, stupid little things. I would love to steal pairs of Nike trainers to make up for the pain of wearing shitty trainers as a young boy whilst the other kids wore the latest fashions. I perfected a trick for stealing trainers. On the display shelf you would have, let's say, three right feet of the same trainer in different sizes. I would ask the shop worker if I could try on a set, so he would pop out to the storeroom to get a brand new box with a pair in it. Whilst he was away I would snatch the right trainer from the shelf and hide it under my seat. The shop worker would return with the pair and I would try on the trainers from the box, but when he turned his head I would slip the left-footed trainer from the box under my seat exchanging it for the right-footed one which I would place alongside the other right-footed one that was still in the box, side-by-side so you couldn't see that they were both for the same foot. I would then tell the shop worker that I never wanted the trainers and he would return the box to the back room. Now with the left footed-trainer under my seat I would have a quick glance around then put it inside my jacket. I would then grab a right-footed trainer from the display and 'Boom', there you have it. I had a brand spanking new pair. They cost over one hundred pounds a pair and I had acquired about thirty pairs. Walking around the town in them I looked like I was sponsored by Nike!

I was dressed in all the latest sports gear with designer labels—all freshly stolen. Back then I used to take pride in wearing stolen things. That was my personality, it was glamorous in my eyes. But I also needed money to go with my new look, so with my team of Warriorz I headed out via Morden Underground Station and hit the smoky city in search of it. We started going into estate agents and stealing 'phones and laptops. We could get around a hundred pounds for a 'phone back then. This was all done by distraction theft, a crime WZ were masters at. Someone would distract the person we wanted to steal from, whilst another of the team was thieving the goods. I preferred to work in and around the London Underground as you could make a quick getaway if things got a bit pepper.

One day someone managed to steal a box of mobile 'phone top-up cards. We ran off and had a look at them. A small handful was worth around six hundred pounds. Sold for half price they earned us three hundred quid. What were we wasting our time stealing 'phones for? We soon came up with the routine of getting off at a tube stop and walking from one off-licence or newsagents to the next. We would peep through the window and behind the counter. Top-up cards were usually held in empty cigar boxes, ice cream tubs or other small cartons. Some of these also had wads of cash in them from the sales of the cards. Once a box was spotted, one or two people would enter the shop and distract the shopkeeper. I was really good at this. I would reach up high for something and pretend I was about to drop it. The shopkeeper would run over to help me and with his back turned my accomplice would lean over the counter, snatch the box and run off. Or it might be the other way around, with me stealing the goods. It wasn't long before we worked out that the best hits were in the ghettos of London.

There would be massive off-licences that were constantly busy and so they held a large number of 'phone cards. The thing is with these ghettos being so rough and ready the shopkeepers were hardened characters. You would have a group of Kurds or Turks running a shop and they really weren't to be fucked with. We must have got off at every stop on the London Underground so you can imagine we got into a few scrapes along the way.

Back then not all shops had CCTV, so we got away with it. Sometimes somebody would get locked in a shop or a big fight would kick off. One day as we were spotted stealing from one place, the shopkeeper grabbed a knife and stabbed one of our lads in the arm. The guy was either Kurdish or Turkish. Another time in Hackney we were spotted stealing a box of top-up cards and ran off. As we sped away somebody dropped the box and the cards went everywhere. As we rushed to pick them up before the shopkeeper arrived we realised we had bigger problems on our hands. A group of Hackney boys had just spotted our prize. They chased us down an alleyway and as I looked back I noticed one of them pointing a gun at us. We legged-it and jumped over garden after garden until some decent Hackney resident gave us a lift out of there.

I had a few guns pulled on me as a youth, even once on an ordinary bus journey. Whilst sitting on the top deck listening to my Walkman and minding my own business a vicious looking geezer produced a handgun and started to polish it. As I looked over at him on he offered to shoot me, but I declined his suggestion. He turned out to be a nice bloke in a strange sort of way. I seemed to attract psychos but knew how to handle them. Another time when I was just fifteen some skinhead geezers, the WK boys' older dodgy uncles (you know what I mean) came down to a funfair looking for me and my Warriorz. They were beating anybody they thought was 706, and they put a sawn-off shot gun up to a fourteen year old white boy accusing him of being me, then they kicked the shit out of the poor sod.

So when it came to stealing, those were the dangers of treading through the ghetto boroughs which are rife with gun crime, but that is where the money was. It wasn't long before we were hitting the jackpot. One day I snatched a box of top-up cards worth two thousand pounds which we off-loaded for near on a grand back in the manor. A few days later, I went into a shop late at night to steal some alcohol, but ended up spotting a big box of 'phone cards and with no-one on the counter I leaned over the length of my body, just managing to reach them, but unaware a security guard was watching me. As I put them in my jacket and made for the exit I spotted him running towards me. Being a cleaver little shit I noticed Tony near the front door so I ran towards him and bumped into him on purpose. All in one movement I shoved the box inside his jacket, pretended I never knew him and shouted out, 'Watch it mate'. I then ran off being chased by the security guard, who was fully unaware that Tony now had the goods. Tony made his exit as I outran the guard. I made my way down the railway and phoned him. He answered and said he was hiding in a bush—and that we were in the money. We met shortly afterwards and counted up nearly five grands worth of cards. For two sixteen year old boys out stealing alcohol we ended up having a good night. We sold them for close on half price, good money for a street kid. One WZ boy made off with eight grands worth one day but was arrested and ended up serving quite a bit of time for his efforts.

I was a street kid day and night. If I was pissed-up and didn't have the energy to walk home whilst I was in Sutton I would go to sleep in the local bus garage. I spent half of my life on public transport, so much so that I should have become a bus driver or a train cleaner instead of a 'menace to the transport system'. I laid there curled up snoring on a out of service bus in the depot dreaming of dead foxes and top-up cards, but I wasn't your average tramp. I was one wearing the newest hundred pound trainers. I never stopped thinking about stealing money or valuables and neither did most of the other lads. If they had a nice pay day they hung up their thieving boots for the night. But whilst they were sitting in front of the TV, I was still out there and getting up to one thing or another.

I walked past an off-licence late one evening and noticed the two Indian shopkeepers outside the premises throwing empty boxes onto the back of a van. I say Indian but they could have been Pakistani or Sri Lankan, but where I'm from we class any Asian-looking person as Indian, even dirty-looking white men! I managed to sneak into the shop without them noticing and peeped out through the window to see if they had spotted me. They were happily carrying on with their tasks. I knew what I was looking for. I lent over the counter and grabbed the red box of top-up cards. With these safely in my jacket I went to leave the shop, but I noticed the back door open which led out to the garden. I thought that would be a better exit, but as I walked out of the door one of the shopkeepers spotted me. Without looking back I ran for it, with the shopkeeper hot on my tail. I crashed into a wooden fence and knocked it down. I rolled over it and ran around the corner and into a dead end. Left with nowhere to turn, the shopkeeper caught up with me and started to throw punches at and wrestle with me. To be honest, they were pretty weak, but I screamed in pain, playing the game. I let him drag me back towards the back exit. As he was dragging me I got caught on the fence which I had knocked down so with quick thinking I pulled out the top-up box and flung it under the it as I continued to scream in pain, but grinning to myself inside. I loved the adrenalin rush at these times. I was Lucky Sevens and and getting away with a lot of things as the madness of it all deepened.

I was held in the shop waiting for the police to arrive. When they did I told them the story of how I was beaten up a week or so ago and I thought the shopkeeper was one of my attackers, so I just panicked and ran off. With no sign of anything on me the officers let me go. I walked off laughing to myself, that crazy voice in my head was saying, 'Well done, son'.

Around three o'clock in the morning I went back behind the shop and there was my prize waiting for me under the fence. This time I was off and gone. After selling the top-ups and including the cash in the box, I made a fair bit. These little earners were nice for a young street kid, although as you grow up you realise it is just pennies in the real world. So many top-up cards were being stolen that the 'phone companies decided to stop selling them. They brought in a little yellow box called a Pay Point where you give the shopkeeper, say, ten pounds and he or she types in that amount and it prints out a voucher for you.

But that didn't stop us street kids from stealing from shops. We just started taking the fresh cash. Where a shop took in so much money that the till would overflow, they often stuffed surplus notes into an old box or even just laid them on a shelf below the till. It was easy money, dirty or otherwise.

We conquered the whole of the London Underground, from Morden to High Barnet, from Chiswick to Plaistow. Those days were crazy, treading in a lot of dodgy manors, getting chased through notorious estates in places like Peckham, hiding from the police in a garden on a ghetto estate in Southall, or engaging in fisticuffs with a Somalian gang in Woolwich. Whilst out and about, I noticed one funny sight in one local borough. As you know, I knew quite a few gentlemen of the road. These tramps and undesirables always seemed to be white. They would dress in dirty, smelly old clothes and crowd around a bench drinking Tennants Super and cheap cider, making a nuisance. Whilst patrolling the streets of Southhall I noticed this exact same image, except that the men were all Asian. It was a picture moment.

It was always great getting back to our own patch though. Sitting on the tube as it pulled into Morden, a Warrior or two down because they had been nicked or were making their own way back by a different route after we had split-up during a chase, I had an overwhelming feeling of joy mixed with relief that I was home and dry.

CHAPTER 12

COME HOME JOE

While these thieving days were passing, my friend Joe was bunked up on his bed in Feltham Young Offender Institution counting-down the days to his next court appearance. I would write to him and tell him about my latest adventures on the streets. I wondered how he felt being locked up for a crime he didn't commit and this made me more and more determined to help him. About six months had passed since Joe was first sent to prison and he was eventually up in court at the end of June 2001 when his legal team made an application for bail and it was accepted, although he still had to face a trial at Croydon Crown Court in October. Keith Gormley pleaded guilty to grievous bodily harm with intent. It meant he would receive a life sentence automatically under the two strikes law as this was his second offence of violence.

I believe that deep down, Joe wanted to turn his back on the life we led on the streets but it was never that easy. When violence, gangs and alcohol are all you know it is extremely hard to just walk away and join in with normal society. I say 'normal' but I mean the working-class system of nine-to-five or studying at college. Our norm was fighting, drinking, stealing and witnessing traumatic events. As a youth you are striving for an identity. Our identities were as crazy youths and we felt respect and love from our peers because of this and that is hard to simply walk away from.

Joe phoned me early in the morning with the news that he was now free for the time being. I met him outside Burger King in Sutton. It had been a long time since we last saw each other—six months was a small lifetime in my young eyes. Considering that we had formerly gone about together virtually all day long, every day on the streets it seemed even longer. We celebrated his release by going brew-raising, all of Joe's thoughts of turning over a new leaf fading as fast as the idea of him doing this entered our crazy heads. We never informed our fellow Warriorz that he was free, planning to surprise them later that evening. Our friendship seemed a lot stronger. We had formed a bond over the last three years and I saw Joe as an older brother. For some reason

I felt we were both living on borrowed time. There was the usual drunken laughter and crazy jokes, but I also felt a sense of sadness coming from him. His court case must have been taking its toll.

Evening arrived and we were by now highly intoxicated. We entered Rose Hill as I had arranged to meet about ten Warriorz along with some WZ girls. Joe put his hood up to hide his face, then I walked up to my mob and they were asking who my new friend was, so me and Joe played a trick on them. I pretended Joe was a total stranger whilst he spoke in a different voice so that the Warriorz didn't have a clue who he was and of course they believed that Joe was still locked up in his cell. This joke went on for a good while until I pulled Joe's hood off and to all of our friends surprise it was good old Joe. Everyone was going mental. They were all so happy and excited that Joe was free and it must have been nice for him to see how many people cared about him. That night we celebrated in the usual manner by getting drunk as skunks, taking binge drinking to the next level. Over the next few weeks I showed Joe my shoplifting and money-making skills including how to steal trainers and also put a bit of money in his pocket from distraction theft. We both had girlfriends at the time and from the slightest glance and our offending apart it might have seemed like we were normal teens.

My new girlfriend was a mixed race girl called Sarah. I started to do a few of the normal things in life such as taking her to the cinema and going out for meals. I really liked her. She brought happiness into my life. I wouldn't say she was my first love as I never knew what love was but I thought highly of her. As she was a pretty girl I received a lot of jealousy and even hate from other local WZ boys who wanted a piece of her. They also hated the fact that I had money. Me and my girl even had matching trainers as I had stolen these for us. I know, how sweet! Her dad saw us wearing them and shook my hand, telling me afterwards to tighten up my handshake. From that day on it has been firm and confident. I keep an eye on any guy with a damp weak handshake, not everyone but a lot of these characters can be a bit dodgy and spineless in my eyes.

Joe now also had a girlfriend and was relatively settled. He was doing some work with his grandad. In fact, WZ was beginning to separate as earning money became the individual members' main agenda. Loyalty and friendship began to go out of the window. Too many Warriorz were turning on each other and the naivety of youth was beginning to be overtaken as people began to realise who their real friends were. I seemed to stay with my group of friends such as Joe and Tony along with one or two others.

Our juvenile enemies from Kingston-on-Thames WK were mainly from the Cambridge Estate, which kept them closer to each other. For a lot of reasons, if you do want to turn your life around, it is much harder if you are all stuck together in the same block. In the case of WZ, we came from different areas, so we weren't automatically drawn together, which for me was a good thing. If we had all been from the same street or estate my life might be a lot different now. I remained friends with my Warriorz but we were now on our separate roads. Other, younger youths joined my gang and I proceeded to take them on missions through London stealing money from shops, and as I was the ringleader I usually received the richest pickings.

One of my friends around this time was a traveller called Wally Smith who was a Romany gypsy. Wally had moved from his travelling site with his family to a street near to where I lived. Now he had the freedom of not being all the time with his own community on a site in Banstead, he took to the local streets to discover what they held in store. That's where I met him and we became good friends.

People like to stereotype the travelling community as dirty or thieves and use negative labels. But how can you judge a community you know hardly anything about? Also, in the criminal world, I've heard the term 'never trust a gypsy'. There are bad apples in every barrel, of course, but from my experience the majority of travellers are kind, loyal and honest people. Wally became a true friend and would have done anything for me as he was fiercely loyal. He was particularly vulnerable out there on the streets as he was used to only mixing with his own kind. His normality was hunting, catching wild birds, boxing and grafting hard from a young age with his father to make ends meet. Quite a culture clash, to go from that to coming-out drinking, stealing and getting up to all types of skulduggery with me.

Wally taught me how to hunt wild animals with a home made catapult and I taught him how to sleeve alcohol. A gypsy armed with a catapult is like me or you being armed with a gun. Wally could shoot down anything with that sling shot. His house was immaculate; not your typical idea of how a gypsy lives. His father was a proud man, who would show me his gold jewellery.

I'm sure gold is a status thing in the travelling community. Wally also had a fascinating collection of rare wild birds in an aviary built at the bottom of his garden.

As time went on and my drinking and mental health became more unstable, Wally's parents became increasingly concerned about him socialising with me. They wasn't used to the police turning up at the front door and with Wally not going home for days on end and eventually being arrested for robbery they tried to put a stop to him seeing me. But for the time being he was hooked on the fast life and would run away from home to be on the streets with me. The settled life just wasn't for them at all, and Wally's family longed to be back with their travelling community.

One time, after a few drunken arguments, me and Wally had a big falling out. The night in question I was virtually paralytic and don't remember what I was saying to him, but he ran off only to reappear with a baseball bat. There I was standing with my cousin Tony in Morden, the next minute I was waking up on the floor. What had happened was that Wally, being a boxer, had given me a knockout punch and, as Tony stepped in, Wally broke the baseball bat in two over his head, a head which must have been reinforced with steel because Tony never even flinched. With me lying on the floor, Tony picked up one half of the bat and chased Wally off up the road. I've got to give Wally a lot of respect. He took on me and Tone single-handed. After that, mine and Wally's friendship was never quite the same again.

Eventually Wally and his family moved back to their own community. He is now somewhere out in Kent and married with children. I still see his family around and it is all hugs and handshakes. His father tells me Wally will always remember those days and often talks about me. They were great fun. I remember sitting on top of a crane in the building site of B&Q in Sutton with Wally singing old Gypsy songs. I was a messed up Asian-looking kid who could speak the lingo with the travellers. Some of the lines I would spit out were, 'Cor dik at the malt ova there' (Look at that stunning girl over there) or 'Cor gel on boy the gavvers are comin' (Hop it the police are coming).

Sometimes it was just me and five other Gypsies, all Wally's cousins. I still see some of them today and we say hello. On a few occasions they've been with other travelling lads who ask, 'Do you know my cousin Wally'. Everyone seems to be cousins and it is respect all the way. I learnt a lot from Wally boy and he's one of those friends I will always remember and respect.

With Wally out of the picture it was just me, Tony and Joe. Surely we couldn't carry on the way we were living. All that self-destructive behaviour must come to an end sooner or later. Was this the beginning of the end? My behaviour was reckless. It is surprising that the local authority never tried to section me under the Mental Health Act. But I was a bit too clever for them or myself at times. Whilst I was under arrest in Sutton Police Station for theft of a mobile phone I started showing symptoms of psychotic behaviour. The sergeant on the day was a black man for a change. For about an hour I was kicking the cell door causing one hell of a racket. He kept on coming to the cell to check on me and this one time he looked through the spy hole he had a right fright. I had cut my arm and covered my face and bald head in blood. Five minutes later a mob of officers rushed in to find the sharp object I had used to do this and also to take my clothing away and leave me with a white paper suit to wear so I couldn't hang myself. They left empty-handed without realising that the sharp object was a sovereign in a ring I was wearing.

I realised I *could* strangle myself with strips from the suit. I simply ripped off an arm and tore it into long pieces then twisted all of these together to make a piece of rope. I used it to choke myself for short periods at a time. I then came up with an idea that would scare the shit out of the sergeant. I ripped off a leg from the suit and made eye holes in it then put it over my face so that I looked as if I was a member of the Ku Klux Klan. To top off my fancy dress costume I cut my arms again with my coin and sprinkled blood over my mask. I must have been the first Asian member of the KKK. When the sergeant saw me he nearly had a heart attack. The thing is, if I was a white boy it would have made some sense, but as I was brown it shocked him even more. He then got onto the phone to the Sutton mental health team and they were down the police station like a shot.

By this time I was all cleaned up and sane again and with a bit of charm towards the psychiatrist she certified that I was well enough mentally speaking and no further action was required. I was put back into my cell and within another half hour was released without charge. As I left the custody suit the sergeant shouted to me, 'You're fucking mental mate, if I had it my way you would be locked up!'

Some of these psychiatrists seemed to me to be more in need of treatment then I was. Didn't they study for years to get to where they were in their careers? Didn't they compare my character with that in some sort of text book? It seemed to be all too easy to pull the wool over their eyes (though I may be mistaken) and I began to think that was why so many loonies slipped through the net and carry out violent acts. Then once these vicious and often brutal crimes happen, that's when alarm bells ring and the big inquires are held, but by then it is mostly way too late. I'm not saying I was going to go out and start butchering innocent people, but I was dangerous and needed help, even if at the same time I was a scared, vulnerable, immature youth. Even back then I always had morals. I never hurt women, children or the elderly. There were times I bullied and there was times I was bullied. I was going nowhere fast. Tell a lie, I was going somewhere very fast and that was back to prison.

I was back on the streets and as self-destructive as ever. Whilst drinking on a Number 93 bus with a group of young Warriorz, I noticed Joe sitting at the front of the bus on his own. I left the young guns at the back and made my way to the front to see my friend. It was broad daylight and nearing the rush hour as the bus headed into Morden. As I spoke to Joe he looked me in the eye and asked me if he should slice his wrist, and me being as mad as ever smashed my bottle of beer over the bus railings and replied by saying, 'Do you dare me?' With that Joe smashed his bottle and we both sliced our wrists in front of all of the other passengers.

We were both wearing matching white Nike jackets and within seconds these were covered in blood. I started to cover my face and bald head. We jumped off the bus in Morden and words can't really describe what we looked like. Just imagine you are making your way home, or waiting for a bus and there in front of you you see two young lads covered in blood throwing each other about, laughing and joking. It was pure insanity. We looked severely deranged. I don't know about Joe but I was seriously disturbed and it is quite shocking for me to think of how nuts I really was back then. Me and Joe then walked around the back of Morden Station and began to fight each other, just a few punches and a bit of wrestling. We thought it was hilarious. We then came up with the idea of boarding a tube to Tooting Broadway to find some more alcohol. I can't believe that during the rush hour we walked back through Morden like that and got on a tube. It makes me cringe to think that was me. We were in Tooting within fifteen minutes

We walked through the packed, cosmopolitan streets and this time actually *bought* our drink. We then came up with the idea of pretending Joe had been stabbed. We made a massive patch of blood on his jacket and he laid outside Tooting Broadway Underground Station. The place was buzzing with commuters and a crowd soon gathered around Joe, and I informed them he had been stabbed in the stomach and I in the wrist. We were smirking to each other as mass panic spread around us. It brings tears to my eyes writing this as it is so shocking to believe we would do such a thing. When the commotion got to be too much I pulled Joe up and we did a runner. We jumped back onto another tube to Morden. As it pulled in I noticed the place swarming with police officers.

We were confronted by the boys in blue. An officer asked why we were covered in blood and we showed him our wrists. We then proceeded to inform the officer that we had stabbed each other. His response was to arrest us both for GBH to each other, which we thought was hilarious. The officer didn't have a clue what he was talking about and we were soon released. We were asked to leave Morden, but within an hour we were back there and a scuffle broke out with a local family.

The police turned up in force and arrested me and Joe for a public order offence. We didn't go without a fight. I was held up against a bus stop and was smashing my head on the glass window to knock myself out. But we soon arrived at our second home, Wimbledon Police Station. I remember an officer getting out a camera and taking photos of my bloody face. Realistically, I stood there and posed, pulling the craziest of faces. I even asked the officer to let me see the flicks to make sure I was happy with them. We were released the next day, and I carried on with my rampage, committing a couple of street robberies over the next few days. There was now a warrant out for my arrest even if I did not know this at the time.

Me, Sarah, Joe and one or two others went to the cinema that evening and watched 'The Fast and the Furious'. I can't say it was one of those films that you remember, but I do recall that it was the last time I would see my best friend Joe alive.

The Lost Boyz

CHAPTER 13

ONCE WE WERE WARRIORZ

That October I was arrested and charged with two street robberies. The following day I was lying on a stinking mattress in a cell in Feltham Young Offender Institution. It felt good to be home. I was on remand waiting to be taken to Sutton Magistrates' Court to plead guilty to both charges. Joe was still awaiting his trial at Croydon Crown Court. The only thing was that he needed me as a witness, but I was now locked in a cell. As we shared the same solicitor, arrangements were made for me to be transferred to the court centre on the day of his trial. Having a witness turn up from prison doesn't look too good, but I was Joe's only hope. The days passed and I would call him on his home 'phone and talk about our cases. Joe would write to me and look out for me on the outside.

The day came for his trial and at seven o'clock in the morning I was ushered over to the reception area of Feltham. All the other kids were going to court for their own cases. I was the only one heading to court for a different reason. Later, I sat in the court cells all day waiting to be called to give evidence when all of a sudden Joe's barrister came down to see me. He told me that the case against Joe had been thrown out and that I wasn't needed. This was really good news and Joe must have been over the moon. I later found out that the barrister expressed concern about my wellbeing. I had become skinny and was a bag of bones with self-inflicted wounds all the way up my arms. But the barrister was concerned about the wrong person, which I will come to.

Keith Gormley was also in court that day for sentencing. He was given a life term with a minimum tariff of three years. As I write this he is into his ninth year of that same sentence. I went back to Feltham and was in a bit of a state. When you're in prison you do not have an inch of control over goings on in the outside world. As I lay there the vultures were circling. Money had gone missing from my stash and every snake wanted to take my girlfriend. The untrustworthy mob had only two things in mind—my money and my missus. So I wrote to Joe and asked him if he could deal with one of these guys for me. The letter went like this:

'Joe you'd better sort out that wanker ... You're my mate ... and I'd do the same for you.'

A week or so later I phoned Joe's home and a strange voice answered. I had called him there for years and was used to him, his brother Dean or mum Denise answering. But this was the voice of an unknown woman and for some strange reason a sense of anxiety washed over me. I asked again for Joe but she said that she couldn't talk and passed the phone over to Dean.

'Hello Dean ... is Joe there please?'

'Joe is dead Justin.'

There was not even a pause on his part. Panic and shock attacked my body. Dead! What did he mean dead?! Dean then informed me that Joe's body had been found by the police in a place we both knew. I went back to my cell and started to cry. I was scared and confused. Joe was my friend, my street brother. It couldn't be true. Why was my friend dead? I couldn't accept it — and if he was dead I want to die too. I was broken, gutted. I was well and truly alone now and I wanted to hurt myself to feel pain, to release the mental anguish I was going through.

My mother had heard the bad news and asked the officers in Feltham to keep an eye on me. They entered my cell and told me that I was being moved into a strip cell so I couldn't harm myself. I lay there in that cell with nothing but my thoughts for company through a sleepless night. I was at my lowest ebb and it was a wonder I didn't keel over and died there and then. I was a nervous wreck.

Joe's funeral took place a week later. I just lay there in my cell under my stinking blanket and cried. I cried for my friend Joe and I cried for the terrible state of my own life. What life? This was not a life. I also cried because I could not pay my last respects in person. But I did write a poem about him which was read out at the funeral. At least my thoughts were there. The chaplain spoke about how this was the one of the biggest turnouts he had seen.

Many of the two hundred or so at Joe's wake were Warriorz, graffiti-writers and other local kids who came to pay their respects. A few WZ boys got a wreath with flowers that spelt out 'BAF', Joe's graffiti tag.

Several weeks passed and a prison officer informed me that some people from the Coroner's Office were here to see me. Coroners? What was a coroner? You would have thought these official visitors would have realised that I was going through a traumatic time, but I was stuck in a visiting room with them, leaving me thinking that here were two nasty, clueless intruders who were probably out to get me. When I entered the room I saw two women sitting there, one black, the other one white. The white one sat with her arms crossed and never looked me in the face, leaving me wondering why she was so disgusted with me. Then the black one fired questions at me.

'Why did Joe kill himself?'

It turned out that when Joe was found he had a letter from me in his pocket and she seemed to be jumping the gun with her theories.

'Why does it say to Joe that you better sort him out ... was you threatening Joe?'

I guessed that in their eyes I was a scumbag who was in prison for robbery, but I was too weak to answer back, sensibly or not. The white lady had had enough of looking at the wall and turned towards me, then tried to murder me with her words.

'Listen you little toe rag, I've got Joe's mother at home in pieces. Her son has been found dead and we want to know why. If you don't tell us we will drag you to court and force you to stand in front of her and give your account'.

With that I ran out of the visits room and was taken back to my cell. I sat there on my own, angry and upset. I had lost my best mate and those two complete outsiders had just tried to ruin me. 'The bitches' I thought to myself. I felt so alone; more alone then I had ever done before. I know Joe had read that letter from me with his mum and thought it was really funny.

Those bitches hadn't a clue. What they were they talking about, 'Did you theaten Joe'? I was good friends with his family after all.

My mum supported me throughout my time inside as ever, but we had always been distant and I couldn't tell her how broken I felt. The days passed and I was escorted to court for sentencing. In the end I got off lightly and was released back onto those rough and crazy streets on Christmas Eve. What a day to be let out of prison. As I left the reception area of Feltham to head to the main gate, I looked over towards Stitch's wing and saw him looking at me through the bars. He shouted to me and asked me to write to him. He must have been heartbroken. I was heading back home to my friends and family whilst he was sitting there looking at the rest of his life sentence.

My mum picked me up from the main gate. With Joe dying I'm sure she thought I would now see some sense and calm down. I made promises about how I was going to change but who was I kidding? I didn't know how to change, plus I was about to enter the streets without Joe by my side. I hadn't even had the chance to mourn for him. The two of us had created WZ and that was was now part of his legacy. If it hadn't been for the two of us there would have been no graffiti in so many places and so many people's lives would have been different. It was hard to face the fact that he was gone and that I must now face our enemies alone. To say events had a negative effect on me is an understatement. I was about to take my pain, self-destructive behaviour and madness to a new level.

When it got to the evening of Christmas Eve I had had enough of sitting around in my mother's house. It was time to see where my friend died. Lying on my bed in Feltham I came up with two different places known to us both and it turned out it was one of these. We used to sit together there and smoke and drink. I can't fully express the pain and horror I felt as I sat there and cried for him. The police were saying that me and Joe had made a suicide pact together but that was nonsense. We had cut our wrists to prove just how crazy we were and to show people we didn't care, but it was just madness and we really did care about what was going on inside our minds otherwise we wouldn't have acted in that way. It was a cry for help, to say to people, 'Look something isn't right here, we are two seriously lost boys'. But even though we walked the streets in broad daylight covered in claret we didn't seem get the help which was needed. This cold, damp place was a place of comfort where I could mourn Joe and still be with him.

My mental health started to deteriorate. I became more reckless and my attitude couldn't have got any worse. I didn't care if I lived or died, whether I was killed or I killed someone else and went back to prison for a long time. I hit the self-destruct button like I had never hit the bloody thing before. I was like a computer which was malfunctioning, a bomb about to explode. I was a lunatic who had just scaled the thirty foot wall of Broadmoor Hospital for the criminally insane. I looked around and was being chased by no-one. I was free to wreak havoc and I had twelve weeks to do so.

I drank like a fish for days upon end. I would sleep on those stairs where Joe died. Some nights I would sit there crying with my shoelaces tied around my neck, but I never had the guts to kill myself. I got some spray paint and did a huge 'BAF' dub on the wall near to where he died, signing it, 'Ill see you at the crossroads, so you won't be lonely, Sevens'. One evening I climbed with a couple of other Warriorz up onto a shop roof where we looked down at the place where only a few months ago there had been so many smiles and so much laughter. As we swigged on our beers, I felt immense anger at what had happened to Joe. I looked over one side of the roof and saw cars and people going about life normally, and then I looked to the other side and could see the place where my friend was found. In an uncontrollable rage I ripped out the leads to the four sets of CCTV cameras and stood over the edge facing the busy streets below. I let out an almighty scream of pain as pedestrians turned to see where the noise was coming from. As they looked up and saw us on the roof, I threw the cameras down onto the street.

With all this commotion going on it wasn't long before blue flashing lights appeared on the horizon. With that my friends ran for it, but I refused to leave. Down there was mine and Joe's private place and I was going to take the roof above it. I climbed over the edge and word soon spread that a boy was about to jump. Crowds started to gather, the police taped off a large area, the fire brigade turned up and a local news reporter showed his face. Warriorz below were putting stones in cigarette packets to add weight and throwing them up to me so I could have a smoke.

I held the roof for an hour as everywhere around came to a standstill. Eventually Joe's uncle, a guy called Mick, climbed up to persuade me to give myself up and come down which I did. At the bottom a couple of Warrior girls were drinking from a Tango bottle. I asked for a sip before I was put into a police car. As I tasted it I realised it was mostly pure vodka and I backed the whole lot in one go. I woke up in an interview room in Wimbledon Police Station with no immediate recollection of what had happened. I wasn't even arrested for throwing the CCTV cameras down into the street. I was just held for my own protection. I was soon released and headed straight back.

Somebody had posted an anonymous letter to the police stating that Joe and me had had trouble with some of our enemies on the night we had cut our wrists and that this had something to do with things. So in my confused state I believed that they had killed him and this was not helped when the inquest jury returned an open verdict. Me and Joe had fought them once, I was sure they wanted revenge and one of them had a record of serious violence. I'm sure you can understand by now just how disturbed I was at the time. I saw the people I suspected one evening and told my friends that it was payback time. I was disgusted with them when they said that they would prefer not to get involved. Where was their loyalty to Joe? So going it alone I picked up a bottle and confronted them including one man who was about twice my size.

'Did you kill my friend you cunt?'

I then chased him and his friends through Morden as my own friends looked on. They got away and I thought nothing more of it, but later as I stood about Morden drinking I sensed someone creeping up behind me. I jumped back in shock. Their leader now had the look of the Devil in his eye as he tried to spray me in the face with superglue. I smashed my bottle on the ground to scare him and a scuffle took place. It seemed now that I was fighting gangs on my own, so I had to up the intimidation factor and become yet more violent. To an outsider my behaviour must have seemed totally irrational, but that was not how I saw it in my twisted mind and blaming someone and attacking people was my coping mechanism. Word soon spread that I wouldn't think twice about using a sharp object to inflict pain on my enemies. This made a lot of would-be predators scared so that they would back off and leave me alone. But I still had my fair share of foes lining-up to take me out. I was totally out of control and walking a dangerous path.

CHAPTER 14

THE TRAIN TO HELL

My behaviour had to come to a stop somehow and it wasn't going to end nicely. It's a shame two innocent men would get hurt in order for me to take a long break from my borough. I had an ongoing feud with a group of boys from Croydon and with no-one by my side it was me against a small army.

I began to arm myself with a meat cleaver for protection, mainly for the intimidation factor. If I was approached by a big group of other gang members I would produce it. I doubted whether any of them would wait to see whether I would use it. I was in a cowering position, stuck within Morden town centre and it felt like enemies were coming to get me from every alleyway and hidden corner. So many people wanted to taste my blood and as the rumours spread about my being ready to use a weapon my enemies didn't come alone but in force. I would get a phone call warning me that the Croydon boys or the Streatham boys were in town looking for me. I would climb onto a rooftop and watch them below as they searched for me unaware that I was spying on them from above.

To my mind at that time my options were, to put it bluntly, death or jail, either of which had to be better then this kind of existence. In a heavily intoxicated state, me and another lad decided to rob someone. My split second plan was to get on the tube and confront a passenger with the cleaver. This was the ultimate act of self-destruction, because I had already learned at the age of fourteen that robbing somebody with a weapon was a serious offence. Plus I was now about to do it in front of CCTV cameras, so it was one hundred percent certain that I was going to be arrested and go to prison for a long, long time. Also, robbing people only usually earned you pennies when I could go out all day around London and earn five hundred quid from things like distraction theft.

'This tube is about to depart, please mind the doors.'

I boarded it stinking of alcohol. As I walked from carriage to carriage, I noticed a man sleeping. He had obviously missed his stop. I approached him and without saying a word to my friend I pulled out my meat cleaver and pointed it towards him. From Morden to South Wimbledon by tube takes around two minutes. Those fateful minutes were drawing to an end as I asked the man for his money as he woke from his sleepy state to see me and my friend standing there and a shiny and terrifying weapon flashing before him. On the spur of the moment and in a state of shock he jumped up catching his chin on the blade as he did so. His blood spurted everywhere. The tube sped into South Wimbledon Station and came to a halt. The doors opened and the man ran for it. He jumped off the tube, most probably thinking that he was running for his life.

You could be thinking that following that chaotic incident we might have thrown the meat cleaver away and run off to avoid getting caught, but that wasn't the case. This was the beginning of the end, remember? As the first victim disappeared another man boarded the train from the platform, in the carriage next to ours. After he took a seat, without hesitation we entered that carriage; my friend going in first. He walked up to this big Asian man who was probably of Sri Lankan descent and put his hands into the man's pockets as I walked slowly down the carriage. As the man spotted me with the meat cleaver, the first victim's blood dripping from the blade, he rightly weighed-up that he was about to be savagely attacked. So he jumped up and made his move. He pounced on me grabbing my wrists to try and disarm me, his fifteen stone frame against my eight stone one. He got me to the floor and was trying to grab the meat cleaver when in the process I cut my hand on the blade. I told you there would be a bloodbath! My hand was now bleeding so I got up, ran off and lived happily ever after on rooftops. Listen, it was far from over. I was in a losing battle and just about to give up when the Asian man managed to wrest the cleaver from my grip. He then stood up, chased my friend down the carriage and had him up against the wall of the driver's cabin as my friend held onto the man's wrists trying to stop him from striking what could have been a fatal blow.

I jumped up from the floor to run for it, but my loyalty wouldn't let me. I spotted a fire extinguisher and without hesitation picked it up and ran towards them, hitting the man over the back and with it head. This did the trick. I then threw the extinguisher to the ground as my friend ran back down the carriage as I followed him, thinking the man was unconscious. But this was now a horror movie that the Devil had put on fast-forward. As I made my way towards the next carriage I looked around and thought, 'Oh fuck'. There was this big and angry Asian man standing there with blue murder in his eyes. I couldn't stop him swinging at me with the meat cleaver. All of a sudden we again seemed to hit slow motion as I begged him to stop. I showed him the fresh white bone hanging out of my hand and said, 'Enough, enough'. With that the tube doors slid open, so me and my friend jumped off and ran for our lives. On the CCTV photos of me running through Colliers Wood Station my feet seem to hardly touch the ground.

I asked a lady on the escalator if there was something wrong with my face and she replied that there was a long wound on my cheek several inches wide. I felt pain all over my body, not realising I had been chopped four times with my own weapon. I ran out of the station and walked the streets for a while as I licked my wounds and then I headed straight for St Helier Hospital. I was so drunk and in so much shock that I didn't even realise the severity of what had happened. It turned out that the first victim had a cut down his chin whilst the second was covered in bruises from the fire extinguisher. I had not only been chopped in the side of my face but the bone connecting my hand to my thumb had been sliced right through. My elbow had also been injured and my thigh sliced into. I lay there on the hospital bed smoking a cigarette, showing everybody my wounds and acting like a complete loon.

'Yeah, this is where he chopped me ... This one on my elbow is a good one.'

The police turned up and I was arrested on two charges of robbery. It wasn't hard to place me at the scene. The CCTV photos of the tube carriage looked like a bloodbath had taken place and it was mostly my blood. I received eighteen stitches down the side of my face, the wound running alongside my jawbone, so that looking at me straight on you can't see the scar, only from the side. An inch lower and I would have been cut in an artery and died, and a couple of inches higher and I would have an ugly scar right across my face. I received five stitches in my elbow and four in my thigh. I had to have an operation on my hand and pins put into my thumb to hold it together, which for weeks afterwards was extremely painful. I also had another ten stitches holding other wounds back together. Wow, thirty seven stitches, that was pretty good work for a self-harmer!

To say the least I was proud of my wounds at the time. But what a messed-up individual I was, a complete lunatic—the wisest man to walk the Earth wouldn't have been able to get through to me. I could easily have watered-down such stories and lied about things saying for example that, 'It was his fault' or blaming other people. I know people who read this book are likely to be shocked and disgusted with me and I will be the first to put my hands up and say that my actions were totally out of order. I didn't deserve to be a free man. I deserved to be locked up for hurting those two men even though the second one seriously hurt me in the process. How can I complain? I thoroughly deserved every wound and every stitch I received. Whatever gave me the right to terrorise two innocent men just going about their ordinary business?

No matter how hard my life was, this gave me no excuse to try to rob people of their hard-earned goods. Street robbery is a scumbag's crime. Any talk of honourable crime is bullshit. All crime has its victims. I don't like it when I hear these so called hard men say such things as, 'The generation of today are absolute scum' or 'In my day there was honour in crime, we would walk an old lady across the road' or go on about how loyal they were whilst at the same time they were cheating on their wives and double-crossing their friends. There is no honour in crime, no honour in cheating, and what comes around goes around, as I know only too well.

CHAPTER 15

PERSISTENT YOUNG OFFENDERS

I had only been free from my last sentence for twelve weeks. As I lay on a blue mattress in a cell in Wimbledon Police Station I wondered what lay ahead of me in life. I knew I would be refused bail at court and probably be held on remand at Feltham once again. A strange sense of relief came over me as I realised that I had escaped that nightmare of an existence on the Morden streets. I was safe and at peace in this police cell, not realising that there was still a long hard road before me where at times I nearly gave up.

So in April 2002 I stood behind reinforced glass with a security guard either side of me as I listened to my solicitor's attempts to convince the three miserable looking magistrates that I should be given bail with the strictest of conditions. It was a vain attempt which failed horribly and I was remanded in custody. I was led down to the court cells and told that I would be on the next bus to Feltham. As I grew bored and more idle I was given a crossword puzzle and a red Biro and when I got fed up with that I started to write my name on the wall in true prisoner fashion. I read other names and messages that had been scratched or written in ink. I felt those other prisoners' pain as they had once sat in this very cell waiting to head back to prison—with messages like, 'Barker and George, no bail 96', 'Fuck this life by Sparky of Mitcham' and 'Back again, gonna miss you Brenda 99'. Next to them it now read, 'Sevens, no bail, fuck this life, Joe RIP'.

Those messages were poetry to me. There was a lot of pain behind them and they came from the writers' hearts, shouting out what was their deepest feelings. Those four walls had witnessed a lot of broken men. In true destructive fashion I broke the Biro in half and removed the tube of thick red ink. I blew through the tube then dipped my blue blanket into the liquid which poured out. I had just made my own super-size felt pen with which I began to write messages on the ceiling. 'Rest in Peace Joe, Warrior for life', getting carried away. As the hours passed waiting for the prison van the walls slowly turned red. I always had to go over the top. It was part of my personality. The cell was now covered in my graffiti and poetic thoughts. I was already in so much trouble that I didn't care about the consequences.

I could hear footsteps getting closer to my cell and realised it was time to jump on the prison bus to head back to my prison home. The almost blind custody officer didn't seem to notice my bloody art work. The sheer cheek of it, no compliments, nothing. That little masterpiece had taken all day.

Back on the bus I looked out of my small window and saw normal people going about their business as I tried to stifle the butterflies in my stomach. I was beginning to feel anxious about what lay ahead. I could have cried there and then as I looked out of that window and noticed the small things that can make everyday life such a pleasant experience. I noticed a father and son going for a casual walk, and a young couple holding hands who looked truly in love. Did they even notice the prison van heading past, did anybody even know I was inside it, or even that I existed? I wanted to be like them so badly. I was in so much pain mentally, but there was to be no warm hug or reassuring words from a loved one on my arrival. Regret took over my thoughts. I was now wishing I had spent more time with my mum and sister, I wanted both of them so badly as well.

'Please somebody help me, please, please help me,' I thought to myself as I cried deep in my soul.

Normal civilisation was fading fast and before I knew it I was back at my second home. I kissed my freedom goodbye. Feltham had cleaned up its act since the murder of Zahid Muberek. The officers seemed more civilised, the food was better, there was no longer a Nazi screw stirring the goulash with his hairy arm. We had televisions and duvet covers. How sweet. Feltham was trying to redeem itself after the pointless and senseless killing of poor Zahid. The whole place seemed to have a different feel to it.

Hold on, I'm sounding as if I liked the place, as if it was some type of holiday camp as the media like to portray all prisons. The material things we were now given made our stay a lot more comfortable but we were all messed up kids and that should have been the main focus of the system, rehabilitation. I'm sorry, but housing all of us together to learn different forms of crime just wasn't healthy. The statistics show that eight out of ten ex-offenders from Feltham commit further offences within about a year of their release. I wished I would be given the chance to commit another crime within a year, but deep down I knew I wouldn't be going home that soon. After my other stays in this five star hotel I'm sure that I had committed further offences within hours of being let out.

The reception officer who would lead you to the main gate to release you was one of those guys that had a lot of high expectations of the youth of today. His parting words would be something like, 'See you soon lads', to which the more or less standard reply would be, 'Eff off'. But I was far away from the main gate. I was locked up with the other street kids doing porridge. I would see an old jail friend and it was all nods or handshakes. When you're a persistent offender and have done say two or three sentences you are guaranteed to bump into the same old faces on the inside. Some career criminals have seen their same prison friends up and down the country in Her Majesty's finest establishments for twenty years and more.

'Do you remember Wormword Scrubs 86?'

'Yeah mate I was on hunger strike with Frankie the Nut.'

'What about Albany 94.'

'Yeah mate those screws hated us.'

It's funny how the nicknames have all changed these days. There used to be names such as 'Tony the Turk', 'Georgie the Loon' or 'Sawn off Steve' who used to go out with 'Carly the Ginge'. These days because of the black cultural scene in London they are things like 'Younger Killer', ' Rinser' or 'Hyper'. This I put down to the influence of rap music from the United States. I could have easily been named 'Justin the Dustbin', but because I was a graffiti-writer I just settled for the name Sevens. Once, whilst sitting in a reception holding-cell, in Wandsworth Prison I listened to these two black geezers comparing their criminal careers. They had both started out around the same time and both had around 150 convictions. As a young man eavesdropping on them I just thought, 'Well you should have thought of a different career, because you're obviously both shit at this one'.

I bumped into a rival graffiti-writer from Sutton on my prison wing. I had known him for years but we never seemed to talk to each other in the outside world. After having a conversation we started to become mates. We hung about together on our wing and couldn't believe we had known each other all of these years but had never really spoken to each other. His graffiti name was Vibe, and there was always discussion between other Sutton writers about who was the best out of me and Vibe. I'm sure that's why we never spoke on the out. Vibe was in prison for spraying a police officer in the face with a can of silver paint. which I thought was kind of amusing, imagining the situation when that officer had to have photos taken of his injuries. I'm sure he wasn't smiling in the pictures.

Me and Vibe made plans about how we would go out drinking and painting together upon our releases. We gained a lot of respect for each other and when I showed him a piece of graffiti I had drawn on paper he told me it was the best he had ever seen. Vibe soon got bail though and I was left feeling lonely on the prison wing. I waited for him to write but the letter never came. Three weeks after his release Vibe was run over and killed by a lorry on our local streets.

Around this time I realised my co-defendant had turned grass on me. This hurt like hell. I read his statement which said, 'Justin Rollins threatened me with a meat cleaver to do a robbery, he also stole the second victim's watch and made me hold it'. I couldn't believe what this scumbag was saying. I had saved his life on that tube and took four chops from a meat cleaver for him. This was so disloyal. He had broken trust and lied as well as grassed. I didn't even know the second victim had a watch stolen. We were both due up in court the following day. I knew I would bump into him in the Feltham reception area and we would have serious words. We were both remanded in Feltham but he was on a different wing to me.

As I made my way into the packed waiting room I noticed my co-defendant looking nervous. There were about fifteen sleepy young offenders in there all getting ready for a day in court. The whole room was silent as everybody stood or sat day-dreaming. I put my hand in my holdall bag and pulled out the statement he had written about me. I then looked at him and said out loud, 'Are you going to grass me up again today?' and with that the whole room erupted with crazy noises and 'Ooohs' and 'Ahhhs'. I passed the statement around for my them to see and with that my co-defendant got milk, sugar and Rice Krispies poured all over him. Or to put it another way, he was lucky to leave that room alive. In criminal terms and in prison, grasses are seen as the lowest of the low and he had to be punished. We stood in Wimbledon Magistrates' Court together as we once again tried to get bail. My co-defendant's solicitor got up to speak.

'My client has just suffered a very traumatic loss, his best friend has recently died and he really needs to be at home mourning with his family at this tragic time'.

I couldn't believe what my ears were hearing. He was trying to use my friend Joe's death to attract sympathy for my co-accused and to get him out on bail. I was filled with rage, but held it in for the time being. We were both refused bail, our case was transferred to Kingston Crown Court and we were then taken back to Feltham. Two days later I spotted him in the education block and cornered him in the IT room. I beat the living daylights out of him, not for grassing me up but for disrespecting my best friend and trying to use his death as a way of escaping the prison walls. As I threw him against a computer I was pulled to the ground by what seemed like ten screws. I looked up and saw fifteen or so inmates bouncing around, screaming wild noises as they thoroughly enjoyed the smell of blood.

My eighteenth birthday came around and I thought I can cry if I want to. I was no longer allowed to stay on the same prison wing and was shortly afterwards moved to the older section which housed inmates from the ages of eighteen to twenty-one. A screw came to my door one day and informed me that the police were at reception and had come to arrest me. I panicked, thinking I was in serious trouble, biting my nails all the way along the long Feltham corridors. In reception I noticed two plainclothes police officers waiting for me. I was relieved when they informed me that I was under arrest for five thousand pounds worth of criminal damage. I thought I was going to be up on a much more serious charge relating to a violent fight I had been in. One of them was the same police officer who had found Joe dead. He often used to chase me and Joe, then the morning after that fateful night he was on duty patrolling the back alleys and had stumbled across Joe's body.

I was handcuffed and escorted to Hounslow Police Station to be processed. During the interview I was shown a handful of photos containing graffiti saying 'RIP JOE' and 'RIP BAF'. Obviously it was me who had done all of it, but I only admitted to one charge. The officer was quite fair because we had a bit of history. I was charged and escorted back to Feltham. To a prisoner this type of episode is seen as a good day out, a break from the sound of banging doors and the smell of prison landings, which often stink of urine.

Whilst on my new prison wing I noticed a prisoner who looked familiar, then it sprang to my mind where I knew him from. He was the guy who had severely bullied me when I first went to Feltham as a vulnerable fifteen-year-old. I looked into his eyes and watched him for a while and he quickly looked away. He realised who I was but the tables had now turned. I wasn't such a weakling anymore and he really didn't want to trouble me. I imagined myself crushing him for the fear he had caused me but I left him alone knowing I had won our battle. He refused to look me in the eye after that.

My time in Feltham was coming to an end once and for all. I was told by an officer that I was to be transported to HM Prison Highdown in Belmont at the top of Sutton. This was an adult prison but had just opened a dedicated wing for young offenders to ease the overcrowding in other prisons. I was quite happy to be moving to somewhere in in my own manor, but I severely underestimated what lay in store. This was no Feltham, no it was a hardcore prison, well at least for me it was.

CHAPTER 16

CRAZY BUSTER AND THE BULLY BOYS

Back on the bus heading for my manor I was going home. I think I will re-write that line. I was back on the prison van heading towards Highdown Prison in Sutton, Surrey, in my own manor. As the van entered my local streets I couldn't help looking out of the window.

'Boy it's going to be a long time until I'm back on those streets,' I thought to myself.

As the van came to a halt I saw the perimeter wall of Highdown and realised that this was no Feltham. It was then holding top security Category A prisoners. After being processed and strip-searched I was given some food and a drink and stuck in a holding cell. It seemed like I was waiting there for ages before I was allocated to the young offender unit. As we walked through the raised prison corridors I felt my anxiety kick in. It was daunting. We entered a cell block which was in the shape of a T, each line of the T containing a prison wing with cells on two sides and with three tiers of landings, one above the other.

The screw unlocked a cell door and told me to go inside, then slammed it behind me. I initially believed that I was in the young offender unit until a big fat hairy bloke on the bottom bunk informed me that he was forty-three-years-old. Don't get me wrong, he was a nice bloke but his feet smelt worse then a sewage farm. He couldn't believe I was only eighteen-years-old. It was against the law for me to be in that cell with somebody of his age but the reality was that no one gave a shit. People would only have cared if my fat cell mate had decided to kill me in my sleep, then it would have been a big thing. When screws break the rules what is a prisoner supposed to do, complain? Well, he can't exactly 'phone the police. Saying that, I remember spending a bit of time in a punishment block once, and you usually get zero privileges there except for one thing—you are always allowed a 'phone call to the Samaritans if you are feeling suicidal. One lad called Kyko, who used to cause the screws many problems, came up with a naughty idea. He shouted out to the block officer, 'Guv, Guv'. The screw came to his cell and answered in the usual manner.

'What the fuck do you want boy?'

'Guv, I feel suicidal, please can I contact the Samaritans?'

'If you're that suicidal, then fucking hurry up and kill yourself'.

Ten minutes later the screw was back with a couple of other evil screws armed with a 'phone. Kyko got what he wanted and began to speak to a member of the Samaritans. He then hung up and tried to 'phone his mates, but this never worked as the 'phone was barred to ordinary outside numbers. He then tried to dial 999 and was successful.

'Could I be put through to the police, please'.

He then informed the operator that he was a prisoner being held in a prison punishment block, and claimed that he was being sexually abused and tortured by the screws. The operator had never had a call from a prisoner before and initially didn't know what to do. In the end and whatever they thought of the merits of his allegation the police turned up at the prison gates to investigate. It was said that the screws now wanted to give Kyko a good hiding but knew they couldn't as the bruises would become evidence. His accusations were false but they triggered a chaotic situation and a bundle of work for the prison service and the police. The prison officers concerned were suspended and Kyko got moved to another jail. I hated the screws and smiled to myself at the downfall of those uniformed Devils.

I remained banged up with 'Uncle Sewage' for around a week before I was relocated to the young offender unit. I happened to get thrown into a cell with a real messed-up kid from north-London named Buster. He was a complete nutjob. There we were sitting in a cell for twenty-three hours a day in the baking heat. I liked Buster but he was the type of person you can only handle in small doses. I had met him before whilst on the out when I was painting Totteridge and Whetstone Underground Station in north-London when he came plodding along asking to use my spray can. One ten minute chat on a station platform three years previously and he seemed to think we were best buddies.

Association periods were used for showering, making 'phone calls and socialising. In Feltham the screws would open your cell door to let you out and then they would normally lock it behind you. And whilst association was in progress the screws hung around to keep an eye on us. My experience of adult jail was totally different to what happened in a YOI, where the screws would come onto the prison wing, open up every door and then piss off and leave you to get on with it. The young offender unit had just opened and I think the Highdown officers didn't have a clue about how to handle us youngsters. They just left us on the wing to our own devices, to get beaten up or robbed by the more hardened young inmates. During one association period a stocky little guy from Deptford came up to me with his sidekick and ordered me to hand over my Phonecards and I politely told him to fuck off.

My naivety had me thinking that was the last of that little episode. I sat in my cell alone writing a letter with the door half closed when it suddenly swung open and four predators walked in. One of them guarded the door and kept an eye out for any screws, but there were none about, too busy I guess sitting on their fat arses drinking tea or coffee and dunking their Rich Tea biscuits.

I jumped up instantly but was thrown back onto the bed, then three of them proceeded to kick the shit out of me. Listen, I could take a beating, but this made me anxious. I had to live with these cowards every day, and could have been attacked at any time. To make things worse, there were two different gangs on this prison wing and Buster decided to start a war with one of them. It got to the stage where we couldn't even go out of the cell because we would have been jumped on and stabbed. He didn't give a shit. At night Buster would sing crazy songs out of the window about these gang members' mothers. People would be kicking their doors and screaming murder. Buster was digging us a double grave and I really didn't want to be buried next to him. It wasn't long before both gangs joined forces to get us. The thing is that I had done nothing wrong and I never did hand over my Phonecards. This type of bullying wouldn't have been allowed to go on over on the adult wings as bullies, grasses and cell thieves were severely dealt with but the young offenders couldn't give a toss for the rules.

The officers must have been aware of the situation as they could overhear the threats being shouted from cell windows. It got to the point where me and Buster had to barricade ourselves in the cell for our own protection. A screw, knowing full well about what was going on, would come along and unlock our cell door and leave the latch on so we couldn't shut it. We would then shove our bunk bed and other furniture up behind the door. Five minutes later we had ten geezers trying to break-in. Once, an attacker nearly got to us, by stretching through the barricade where there was just enough space to manoeuvre his left arm. He was holding a toothbrush with razor blades melted into the end of it, swinging it hopelessly in our direction. Buster's character was in full swing as he taunted our attacker by slagging off his family and kicking the guy's arm. The screws turned up to break up the commotion and I yelled out, 'Guv, lock our door, for fuck sake'. Incidents like this went on for several days so that me and my cell mate were lucky to be alive by that point. I couldn't take this shit anymore and needed to escape what was becoming a living hell.

I told Buster that I was going to cut my arms with a razor to get myself removed from the wing and hopefully land somewhere safer and more comfortable. He didn't want me to do this as he would be left to face the enemy alone, but I had no time to stand by his side whilst he caused more trouble, and after all it was Buster who had got me into this mess. I grabbed a razor, made some deep cuts on my arm and then covered my face with blood in true Warriorz style. I pressed the buzzer and an hour later the screw came traipsing along.

'What have you done that for Rollins, you knob?'

I was then escorted to the hospital unit to be patched up. It was totally different to the young offender wing and a lot less hectic, just one long corridor which had cells on either side of it. I was patched up by a doctor who told me that I wasn't allowed to stay on the healthcare unit as there wasn't a separate part for young offenders. Apart from me, there were just adults in there, about twenty of them in all. I was put into a cell to rest for a while before being taken back to Hell.

I sat in the cell where I was resting and it felt so peaceful. You could have heard a pin drop it was that quiet. On the cell door you even had a flap that remained open so that the nurse could pass your medication through it. I felt totally relaxed down there, there were no televisions in the cell but I could handle that. At least I was safe. I dreaded being taken back to the young offender unit but my fears came true and within the hour I was re-allocated to my living grave with Buster. As I lay there and listened to the usual screaming and shouting I longed for the quiet of the hospital unit.

Two days later, I thought, 'Fuck it', I'm going back to healthcare wing no matter what'. So I cut my arms and using my own blood wrote Devil symbols across the cell walls—and with that little trick was soon taken back there. I lay in my new cell with my feet up feeling like a king and thinking, 'This is the life!'

The doctor had to make a choice. Keep patching me up and sending me back to Hell or break the rules and let me stay under his care. He chose the second option.

CHAPTER 17

LOONY BIN NUMBER ONE ....

I was temporarily at peace in the quiet of my new cell, just little old 'Justin the Dustbin' and nineteen adult prisoners. These healthcare units are meant to hold prisoners who are physically ill and occasionally mentally-ill ones too. But from my experience they tend to just hold nutcases, loonies, weirdos, fruitcakes, psychos and severely dangerous men. As I lay there feeling at home I never noticed I was surrounded by complete madmen. Considering my own history, it seemed that I would fit right in and I did. It was like one of your parents giving you a bit of courage when you felt anxious about playing with the other kids in the park when you didn't know them.

'Go on son, go and play with the other psychopaths and freaks, make sure you enjoy yourself.'

The healthcare screws seemed to be a more decent bunch then your regular prison officers, although from the start they made it clear that I wasn't wanted there. They saw me as just another troublesome young offender. But my youthful ways seemed to bring a bit of sunshine to that place. I wasn't your average nutter who had bludgeoned his victim to death with a blunt instrument. I was a hyper-active, messed-up kid who would stupidly question a paranoid schizophrenic about why he had killed his victim. The guy I put this question to was your typical mental patient from a Hollywood movie. About fifty-five-years-old, six foot five, arms so long his fingers nearly dragged along the floor, he had a yellow beard which almost touched the ground. I'm sure he had the odd bird nesting in it. He was a Category A prisoner, which meant he was highly dangerous and a top security inmate. He had randomly attacked a lady and stabbed her to death. Seventy-seven times. I sat in the association room next to him with the other loons and my erratic mind fired questions at him.

'Why did you stab her seventy-seven times? ... By the way I'm Sevens, nice to meet you.'

His response would be to run off holding his ears, screaming and shouting to himself. You could say I was dicing with death, but I always had a need for a bit of danger. It appals me how I could do this and how the officers let it happen. But for the time being I was enjoying myself and this patient looked like a pussy-cat compared to my other new mates. There were some seriously disturbed men down there and a lot of smelly ones too. One inmate, who used to walk around his cell constantly, had a serious hygiene problem which resulted in the officers getting togged-up in paper suits and masks before dragging him to the showers. But the smell never went away. Before long they found out why. He had been holding slices of bread out of his cell window to attract the prison pigeons that were doing time. Unlike us though, they also faced the death penalty. He would grab hold of a pigeon and pull it into his cell. Then he would bite the head off and store it in his pillow case. The screws made the gruesome discovery of a sackful of pigeon heads whilst cleaning out his cell. One woman officer couldn't help but spew-up her breakfast and I don't blame her. When the story went the rounds everyone was put off their food for a while. We named that little episode 'One Pigeon Flew over the Coo-Coo Nest'.

The screws and nurses began to like me, because although I had my problems I would still speak sense to them. But my experiences left me wondering how they coped with what they saw day in day out down on that unit. My first experience of the gated-cell was when I decided to slice my arms constantly for a few days. The doctor feared I would end up killing myself so he allocated me to one of the gated cells on the unit. These cells were also known as 'cages'. A nurse or screw would do shifts sitting outside the cell watching you constantly. I was so skinny I would climb to the top of the gate and put my legs through the bars half-way up, sitting there like a monkey in a tree. My next door neighbour at the time was Ned, a big, forty-year-old geezer from Shepherds Bush in west-London. Outwardly, he seemed seriously mentally-ill. I found out that he had covered himself in his own faeces and then tried to hang himself. I tried to talk to him but he never really responded. Then one day whilst sitting next to him in the corridor he suddenly began to speak.

He needed to get something off of his chest. He told me that he wasn't really mentally-ill, but that it was all a big act. He was pretending to be disturbed so that he would be sectioned under the Mental Health Act and not receive the hefty prison sentence he was looking at for armed robbery. He explained to me that a *real* mental institution was the stuff of dreams compared to your ordinary prison. I listened and thought, 'Why not, I'll have some of that too.'

I followed in Ned's footsteps and pretended to be mentally-ill, but it didn't work that well. One day I decided that I was going to cover myself in my own shit. You are probably thinking, 'How disgusting is that?', but in prisoner terms deception tends to happen a good deal. And to be honest it was quite an experience to say the least. I picked up my log and began to wipe it over my face, head and body. I then rang the buzzer and said to the screw, 'I've covered myself in shit … Can I have a shower please.' It wasn't exactly the best portrayal of a disturbed prisoner, Ned's was quite a performance and far more likely to get him nominated for an Oscar.

As me and Ned became mates he suddenly started to come out of his shell. I was making him laugh with my crazy antics and my jokes, such as grabbing a fat old paralysed paedophile by the handles of his wheel chair and running at speed with him down the corridor as he screamed for me to stop and with me howling like a wolf—then again in the other direction and with Ned laughing his head off. The screws laughed as well. No one likes a paedophile and this particular sack of shit was lucky I never bumped into him when I was in a violent frame of mind, like someone else did one day in the showers. Sometimes we were a couple of dribbling loons who burst out laughing but didn't know what we were laughing at.

Indeed, my new home was swarming with loons who came and went. But even though the place was full of deranged and sometimes dangerous individuals I never felt unsafe. That is until one episode with a massive black geezer from Tulse Hill. He looked quite normal so I started to speak to him and he was friendly towards me. A day or two later he sat beside me and asked if I was a Braveheart. I told him I didn't have a clue what he was going on about, but he carried on accusing me of being one. Realising he was a complete nutter I tried to avoid him. The next day whilst in the healthcare exercise yard, I noticed he was staring at me. I was lucky to be standing up, so that I could see over the others to what was coming. He walked over to me and in slow motion pulled out a knife made from an empty tuna can and lunged at me with it. I ducked and ran away from him. Within minutes there were half-a-dozen screws on top of him. After that little incident I was much more cautious—for a day or two that is.

When you're a remand prisoner you are allowed visits from people quite regularly. Convicted prisoners have to send out visiting orders to their friends and families, but remand prisoners' contacts on the outside just phone up and arrange to visit. This means that any old person can turn up; as I was about to find out. I sat in the packed waiting room hoping for one of my friends to turn up. I waited and waited but couldn't see him. I then noticed an Asian-looking man walking towards me. I thought, 'I don't know you, why are you heading in my direction?' I then realised it was the geezer who had chopped me up with my own meat cleaver. He ran towards me and started to throttle me. Only winding you up, but I have just highlighted something that could have easily happened because any old person can just 'phone up and visit you whilst you're on remand. Anyway, my victim from the incident on the tube didn't show-up, but another Asian-looking man did.

This stranger sat in front of me and I asked who he was. He replied that he was my dad. What a head fuck. I was already mentally unstable, then this guy turns up to screw me up a bit more. I hadn't seen the coward since I was two-years-old. I gave him the once over and realised that I most probably got my good looks from my mother. Well, if looks could kill he would have been lying there in a foetal position on the visiting room floor. I asked him what he thought of me being in prison and he crossed his arms and told me he wasn't happy about it.

'Well, sorry dad, I haven't seen you for sixteen years!' My anger boiled up inside of me. He also said that if I had been brought up with him none of this would have happened. Basically, after sixteen long years I thought he was trying to put down my mum. He left her to bring up two kids on her own and settled with another woman and a further two kids. My half brother and sister were brought up in a stable and happy home whilst our lives were so different. My mum brought up me and Jemma by herself in a council block, even if she wanted a better life for us, which she tried for by working and saving enough money to buy a place for us. The emotional side may have been light, but she stood by us. My dad never tried at all, plain and simple.

This man was playing on my mind. Why didn't he just go back where he had come from? I went back to my cell angry and disturbed and started cutting my arms to feel physical pain instead of the mental anguish of it all.

A week or so later I was due up in Kingston Crown Court for a plea and directions hearing. I pleaded guilty to one count of robbery and one of attempted robbery. My solicitor recommended that I should have psychiatric reports prepared on the state of my mental health before the judge sentenced me and he agreed that they should be completed within the next six weeks.

Back in the loony bin the fun continued. By this time I had totally blown Ned's cover concerning his attempts to get himself certified. He virtually had one foot in a mental institution before I turned up but as the weeks passed he was laughing and joking more and more because of me and the nurses. They eventually noticed he was well again and moved him back to a normal prison location. He must have been really pissed-off that I had arrived next door to him whilst he was acting-out the role of a madman.

Somebody was now about to turn up and almost destroy the peace of my new little home. I heard a familiar loud voice down the corridor as I lay in my cell so I jumped up and looked through the flap. Yeah, you guessed it, it was Buster. I shouted to him and he informed me that things had started to get really nasty up on the young offender unit, so he had carved the word Demon into his arm and had been placed on the healthcare unit. I wasn't too happy that he was down there with me as he was a complete troublemaker. It wasn't long before he grabbed hold of the fat paedophile in the wheelchair and began running around the unit with him. Even though I didn't want him there I was crying with laughter as the paedophile screamed for help.

I was in and out of that gated-cell week in week out and my new next door neighbour was in the Premier League when it came to self-harming. This nutcase had pulled out a razor blade and sliced his own neck with it. He was deranged and lucky to be alive, He had fifteen staples holding it all back together. I realised I was an amateur when it came to self-harming, but unlike Ned this guy never gave me any thoughts of following in his footsteps. One day I did cut a few really deep wounds with a razor blade, initially because I thought I would be taken out of the prison to St Helier Hospital to be patched up and that would give me the opportunity to have a little nose around my old home town. But this plan didn't work, the doctor took me straight to the medical room and stitched me up there and then. He also started to feed me medication to stabilise my mood swings.

What a fool I was, he was giving me Olanzapene, which is used for treating psychotic patients, and some other drugs. They made me feel slow and took away my sense of humour. But taking those pills was like somebody handing me their last Rolo compared to one mixture I was given. I didn't think twice about taking this liquid concoction but after falling into a deep sleep an hour or so later when the door opened for association with other prisoners I tried to get up but couldn't. My head was having a spasm and stuck sideways down on my left shoulder. My tongue was hanging out and my hip was bent inwards so I couldn't walk properly. When I did manage to get up, I could only stumble around the unit. I didn't have a clue what was going on. I walked around like a cripple begging the nurses for help, my whole body bent double.

I looked seriously disabled but the nurses ignored my muffled cries. 'So this is what they do to real mental patients to shut them up,' I thought. I eventually lay on the corridor floor having a fit whilst a nurse walked past and left me there. After rolling around for a while, I managed to get to my feet and hold onto the wall to balance myself. I dragged myself to the 'phone and with all of my fighting spirit pulled out my Phonecard, stuck it in the slot and dialled my mum's number.

'Mum … mm … mm … they're drrrug … ing …mee …ca … cann't … move, hhhelp mmmee.'

With that I couldn't manage anything more and hung up the 'phone. Worried sick, my mother called the prison demanding that they take care of her son. Fifteen minutes later the nurses picked me up, one on either arm and put me in my cell. I was given a further dose of the liquid mixture and two sleeping tablets and with that I fell into a prolonged sleep. I woke half-way through the next day feeling a great deal better. I got no apology from any member of staff for what had happened the day before.

When you enter a prison you become nothing but a number. Every day dignity goes out of the window, you get strip-searched and you could be sitting on the toilet when all of a sudden your cell door opens, prisoners and visitors walk past and see you wiping your arse. You get talked to like you are nothing but a piece of shit, sometimes by sadistic screws who get a buzz out of using their power to humiliate people. If an officer doesn't like you for some reason, he can just take the mail that your family have sent to you, rip it up and throw it in the bin. If you were to be brutally beaten by officers and one of them was sickened by what he or she had just witnessed their colleagues doing, there is a slim chance they would back you up. At the end of the day they are the prison officers and you are an inmate. Some screws do actually care about the inmates but in my experience they are in the minority. The media loves to say how prison is easy, but from my experience the animals are treated a whole lot better at Battersea Dogs Home.

After my dodgy medication episode I started to kick-off all the time. I would smash up my cell, cut my arms and cause mayhem. The screws would come into my cell, wrestle me to the ground, drag me through the corridor, take my clothes from me, stick me in an unrippable gown and throw me head-first into a strip cell. This was supposed to be somewhere where you couldn't harm yourself. The bed was a big wooden block glued to the ground, with a plastic mattress on top of it. Apart from that you had a toilet and a sink with buttons instead of taps. I swore to myself that I could still harm myself. I blocked the sink with tissue then kept on pressing the buttons, I flooding the cell as much as I could. I had nothing on except for this unrippable gown and my feet were nearly ankle deep in water. I then grabbed the mattress and threw it onto the floor soaking it. Then I started to slam it against the cell door. It made an almighty bang each time, over and over again. With that the screws turned off the water supply to my cell. I could see eyes peeping through the spyhole. I would see that Devil's eye regularly during my prison sentence.

'Yeah, you're the fucking master, I'm the animal,' I shouted.

I then started to chew on the gown trying to force a hole in it, but the material was so thick it was hard work. But I was pumped up with rage and anger, so I chewed and chewed until my mouth was bleeding. I noticed a tiny hole appear—it was working at last. The Devil-eye was still at the spy-hole but I carried on until eventually the hole was big enough to get my big toe through it. With every bit of Warriorz blood I had left, I stuck my finger through the hole as well and pulled with all of my strength. I went flying as the gown tore, and I let out one almighty scream as I wrapped a loose piece of the material around my neck. The cell door flew open and the screws were on top of me taking the piece of ripped gown before I could hurt myself. I could feel that I was about to pass out as they cut it from around my neck. I lay there gasping for air. I smiled at the officers. I was buzzing, I was a complete loon, but I loved the feeling of damaging myself, I needed help.

The officers gave me some new clothing and hauled me into the gated-cell to be kept under twenty-four hour observation. A lot of the other inmates were quite concerned about me. They thought I was going to end up killing myself. But a few days later I was back to normal—until the next time.

CHAPTER 18

SELF-HARMER CENTRAL

The pressures of serving time on the healthcare unit were starting to get to me as I witnessed more and more young offenders passing through my hideout. First it was Buster with the word Demon carved into his arm. Following his and my example, there was a mass migration of young offenders to the unit as several other lads were brought in with self-harming marks and Satanic words or symbols carved into their flesh. One guy from the Sutton area had the words 'Devil Forever' carved into his chest. Other vulnerable youths had clocked on and wanted to make new homes like ours. Like some sort of sick fashion statement, it became cool to have an evil legend carved into a part of your body.

A lot of these young offenders stayed for only two or three days, as they were seen as a nuisance and not a real threat to themselves. On the other hand, I was allowed to stay as I had shown enough craziness and done enough self-harming to earn me a bed there. Some of these young offenders were so vulnerable it was amazing. In the evenings one lad used to press his cell bell just to say 'Goodnight' to the screws. It was meant to be used in case of emergency. Even if it was an emergency, sometimes it might take a screw an hour to check on you, so if you really had sliced your wrists deep enough you could be dead before anyone arrived.

Whilst sitting in my cage one evening I noticed a new young offender being dragged through the unit by a handful of screws. The poor guy looked to be in a real state. He was placed in a strip cell for the night. In the morning I sneaked out to see who he was. His name was Jimmy Penfold, a traveller from the Sutton area. I passed some tobacco to him through his cell flap and moved on quickly. A few days later he was allocated to a cell on normal location. Me and Jimmy hit it off from the start as we knew some of the same people on the out. I told him about my plans to be sectioned under the Mental Health Act to avoid a hefty prison sentence and he told me he planned to do the same. He was in prison for taking part in the Millwall football riots, where dozens of police and their horses were injured, so he was looking at a bit of time as well. We once sneaked into the screws' office and stole two pencil sharpeners. We planned to injure ourselves with the blades as part of our plan. We were grassed up by another prisoner though and the plan failed.

There were now several of us young offenders trying to get sectioned. While other kids our age were trying to gain entry to a college or university we were hoping to get into a mental institution. Funny how life turns out, isn't it? I came up with the tactic of burning a hole through the cell light cover and smashing the bulb to use the glass to self-harm, but the glass seemed far too weak to use. We were having our shaves supervised by prison officers to prevent any of us cutting ourselves with the razors, so we had to come up with different tactics. One day, I got hold of a large plastic prison bin-bag and covered my top half with it whilst in the cage. I then tied a shoe lace around the neck so that I would suffocate. It was lucky I was on constant watch. I'm lucky to be alive as the number of times I self-harmed in one way or another was extraordinarily high. Okay, I say I was trying to be sectioned but at the same time these acts were a cry for help from a seriously disturbed individual with deep emotional problems. I'm sure some of the nurses and screws knew this was the case.

So me and Jimmy waited for our reports to be done, and when the day arrived for our assessments we would have to be on form and make the right impression. The psychologist was going to be the man to dictate our futures.

As the days go by when you are serving time in prison you think less and less about the outside world. Late at night you might dream about being free, but during the day you fall into a routine that stops you thinking about freedom at all. I would think of being free at times and about my life outside, but as the days slowly passed I began to feel like a complete stranger to my family and friends, which was partly also due to my being such a disturbed individual. I knew that on the outside I was a complete mess and if they had opened up that gate there and then I would have been right back in the thick of my horrible existence on the streets. So as I lay there thinking about my life on the out, I was happy I to be safe and sound in a cell. I got two meals a day and even though my life on the healthcare was disturbing at times and often hectic it seemed to be a lot more peaceful then life on the south-London streets. It is funny how you adapt to an environment and make it your home. On the out I used to sleep wherever I could lay my head, so being away from my family wasn't my main problem. Confusion was the biggest enemy.

I was so lost in this crazy mind-set that I didn't know who I was anymore. That is why I was such a stranger to my loved ones. I had created a monster. I was lost in my madman personality and it hurt like hell. I was actually scared to look in the mirror and see my own eyes staring back. Those eyes seemed dark and crazy and they would freak me out. On the one hand I was a kind loyal person and on the other I was a complete liability. I was also at the time scared to talk about my deepest feelings and problems. So being there in a smashed-up cell dripping blood, screaming at the screws, was my way of saying, 'A little help here, please.'

I had been on this wing for a few weeks and started to feel at home. The only thing was that we never had TVs like the rest of the jail and you would be lucky even to get a prison radio. So the days were long, lying on your bed for up to twenty-three hours. I was lucky. I got a radio. Listening to the news, I heard the presenter talking of a horrific murder with the killer on the loose.

'Do not approach this man. Contact the police immediately.'

I kept hearing this broadcast on every hourly news bulletin and was wondering what this guy had done to cause such a media frenzy. A few days later I was reading the *Sun* newspaper and came across the story of a man who had killed his friend before dismembering his body and dumping parts of it in his local area. He had skipped the country but been caught sitting in a park reading an English newspaper. In the next few days he would be face extradition to the UK. Apart from the gory details, I thought nothing more of it.

Then one afternoon during association, Buster came storming up to me to say that the killer from the news had just landed on the wing. Wow, in prison terms this guy was a celebrity, a Category A prisoner, highly dangerous. My young and foolish mind became excited. Two minutes later I poked my head out of the door and saw the legend himself, let's call him Chopper, walking down the corridor seeming only too happy with himself. I called out and invited him round to my cell. He was in his late-twenties—a top security prisoner, and he was now sitting completely unescorted in a cell with a an impressionable eighteen-year-old. He could have closed that cell door and cut off my head off as he had allegedly done to his victim. Well he didn't. I pulled out a newspaper and showed him the story and picture of himself and he signed it 'Happy Chopping' followed by his name.

Over the next few days we talked a lot. He was kept in a gated-cell on suicide watch, where I would talk to him through the bars. I came up with the idea to self-harm and get put in the cage next door. It worked and we become next door neighbours. Have you ever had the thought that one of your neighbours, the weird one that never talks to anybody, is some kind of killer? Well mine was. The thing with these cages was that given their position me and Chopper could talk and even play cards. I soon learned his story, about how one night after a hard drinking session with a friend an argument broke out between them. He had grabbed a hammer and repeatedly beat the friend around the head with it until part of his brain splashed over the walls and the ceiling. What he did next was something you don't even see in a hardcore horror movie. He sawed up his victim and distributed the parts around the town.

When he woke up a few hours later there was a smell of burning and he ran over to the oven to discover one of his friend's limbs on a baking tray! He showed me the police drawing of the layout of the house. In one of the rooms was a picture of the limb with a fork sticking out of it! The archetypal neighbour from Hell might not, I guess be everybody's cup of tea, but at that time in my life I was in complete awe of him. I craved danger and madness from a young age, so what better then a human butcher-cum-masterchef to engage with? You would think even the most disturbed of people would give such a person a wide birth. But I didn't and I just couldn't wait to tell people about my new celebrity acquaintance. I even borrowed his jumper to go and meet my visitors.

Around this time I was told that Joe's father who was himself a prisoner, had been allocated to Highdown for a few weeks to receive visits as his usual abode, Whitemoor Prison, was so far away from his family and friends that they had been finding it very hard to see him. Joe's father is Razor Smith, a hardened, respected and feared armed robber-cum-villain from the south-London streets who has spent many years in Her Majesty's prison system. I saw this respect first hand when a screw asked how come a disturbed little runt like me knew someone like Razor. I saw the screw's attitude change as he became no longer the bully boy. He too had a respect for Razor and he would never have dared talk to him like shit.

Prisoners are not usually allowed private or in-cell visits from other prisoners unless they are family. But due to Razor's credentials and my unstable mind they thought it would do me some good to meet him in the prison chapel, which we did by coincidence on Joe's birthday. I walked in anxiously and saw him sitting there and I remember thinking just how much like Joe he looked. Our next visit was in the cage on the healthcare unit. I did wonder what Razor must have thought of me being in such an environment, but I never asked him about this as it was quite the norm for me. As we wandered outside the cage, Chopper came walking along and I introduced Razor to him. He knows the prison system inside out and was quite amazed that his son's skinny, mixed-up friend had been allocated alongside such an individual. But after doing as much time as Razor has, I'm sure that his amazement didn't last long. I'm sure he knew as well as anyone about how dysfunctional the system could sometimes be.

So we sat down for our visit in good surroundings: three walls, an iron gate and the odd psychotic killer walking by having a nose. I remember an officer walking in and offering to make Razor a cup of tea. This is something I had never seen before, a screw offering to make a prisoner a cup of Rosy Lee? I thought, 'Wow, Razor's got these screws running around for him.' At the time he had started to write his autobiography and this began to inspire me to try to write something down as well. I only ever remember Joe talking about Razor a few times. He once showed me a magazine with some of his father's writing in it. Back then, being the loud unstable character that I was, if I had had a dad like Razor I would have broadcast it all over the place, but Joe was quiet about his dad and only told me privately about his reputation. Razor was later taken back to Whitemoor. We shook hands and promised to keep in contact. He was kind to me and it made me feel closer to Joe.

Me and Jimmy Penfold were informed that our psychiatric reports were being done by the same doctor on the same day a couple of weeks later. We made our preparations by self-harming and acting crazy. Jimmy would walk around with medicine cups stuck to his face and I would cover myself in my own blood. When the day of reckoning came Jimmy went in to get his reports done before me and when he came out he signalled to me to be at my best.

I entered the room and sat in front of the doctor who fired questions at me for an hour or so. I thought I had done quite well with my acting, but I later found out that I was not going to be sectioned under the Mental Health Act. What I *was* told was that the doctor had diagnosed me as having a borderline personality disorder. They could have said anything as I never had the slightest clue what that label meant, and although the system likes to place you in pigeon-holes they don't like to tell you what it means or how you can seek help. So I wasn't going to a cushy nuthouse. I was looking at a long prison sentence.

Jimmy was a lot luckier. Or was he? He did get his wish to be sectioned. Years later, when I was a free man again, I bumped into him around the manor and we caught up on things. He didn't stay free for too long. He was soon arrested and placed back in a local prison. I wondered what his plan was this time. Late one evening, alone in his cell, he decided that enough was enough and he committed suicide. When I was told about his death my mind was a long way from the days of the healthcare unit. I can't say I was surprised and I will always remember him, but mostly for the times I saw him on the out rather than a prison.

When my day for sentencing arrived, I climbed aboard the prison van to make the short journey to Kingston Crown Court. I stood in the dock and looked across at the public gallery and saw my own and Joe's family. The judge asked me to stand up and I rose to my feet staring deep into his eyes to see if he gave anything away.

'Justin Rollins, I have read all of the reports on you and can see that you are a very unstable, violent character. The robberies you committed were extremely brutal ones and for that reason I can only hand down a lengthy custodial term. I sentence you to four-and-a-half years for robbery and a further four-and-a-half years for attempted robbery … to run concurrently. You may take him down'.

I thought I had received nine years but as the two sentences were to run concurrently it was half of that. I guess I was shock. To an eighteen-year-old a sentence like that represents a lifetime. As things then stood, I would have to serve at least three years before I was eligible for release. I would be nearly twenty-one by then and I had committed these offences as a seventeen-year-old. My family and friends started to crying for me in the public gallery, which didn't help my butterflies as I was led away. A few days later it hit me hard and I broke down in my cell and cried my eyes out. Three years and more in that environment! I was so messed up and confused. Why did I do those things? Why was I in this mess? I looked in the mirror and shouted at myself.

'Who are you Rollins?!'

I punched the mirror until my knuckles bled. I lay there in my cell cold and alone and I dwelt more and more on the label they had given me.

'What does borderline personality disorder actually mean?!'

EPILOGUE

Looking back over my book and my life leaves me in a dark place. In fact it sickens me and I am not afraid to say that I am deeply ashamed, especially about the violence and other crimes. Did I really live a life like that? Was it the real me? Then I look in the mirror and see the scars and tattoos expressing my anger and pain and realise it did happen and, yeah, it was me. And I'm glad I don't lead such a life now. But I will be judged on my actions, and I guess that there will be people who want to write me off altogether or think I should be locked up and the key thrown away.

Whatever, the past is history and I must look forwards now. I have served my time and punished myself already with all the self-harming, alcohol abuse and lack of concern for my own welfare, but now it is time for me to move on and to try and help other young people to avoid, or get out of, such a lifestyle whilst they can. If you lived a childhood like mine you might well have scars—physical or mental—and even those of you from the most secure backgrounds will I think understand that childhood is a different world, where all kind of influences come into play. We are all at risk of going off the rails, you only need to keep up with the daily news to see this. You might then move on, grow up, become wise, but you will always have the memories, whatever they are, the flashbacks and the occasional dream, good or bad. Mine were often the stuff of nightmares. The thing is that you can either sink or swim. I'm not a good swimmer, more of a paddler but whatever you may think I'm going forward and staying positive.

Do I have regrets, now that is a question? Of course I regret that some of my friends died or that there were innocent victims. But I have no regrets about the fact that the life I led on the streets made me the person I am now, tough, resilient and a survivor. I can only say that I don't recommend my kind of past to others. I have already said that I am thoroughly ashamed of some things, but now I try my damned hardest to hurt no-one, to be trustworthy and a man of my word, and never ask for anything.

Underneath all the craziness of the past I was for anyone who could have found it a nice kid, but in the world I knew kindness was seen as weakness, one false move and you were mincemeat; the enemy could smell blood at the first sign of weakness. I remember I was out on a street robbery mission with my fellow gang members. There was traffic queuing on a busy street, an old man had fallen down and he was lying in the road with his shopping spilling out. My fellow Warriorz did not run to help. I looked on him and froze, I wanted to run over so badly to help the poor guy, but I feared my friends would laugh at me for doing the right thing. These days I would be the first person to help, not because I've turned into some sort of do-gooder, far from it, but because I treat people with proper respect no matter who they are— and to do that I first have to respect myself. As a youth I did not have one ounce of self-respect and little or none for anyone else beyond my gang. In fact I hated myself. I would harm myself and I would harm others.

I served three and half years in prison, and I did it the hard way. I got punished physically and mentally, and the mental part of it creeps back now and again, but I am a fighter and I will march on always. A phrase I try to live my life by comes from a song a friend wrote: 'I never negotiate with negatives'. You think negatively and you will be surrounded negative people, down-and-outs and losers, and odds on you're soon in a downwards spiral yourself. Surround yourself with winners and you are more likely to become one yourself.

Then there's the saying 'never judge a book by the cover'. I get judged quite often on my appearance. Nowadays I am sixteen stone in weight, train at the gym four or five times a week, am heavily tattooed, covered in slashes and scars, have a shaven head and several white gold teeth. Yeah, sounds like a monster! I have also been told that I can sometimes be a fearsome character but gentle with it.

As I said earlier, we all have a past and we are only human. I love the old ways, the old couple holding hands, the opening of doors for ladies, the smiles, the handshakes. You will have read in my book about the dark side of my generation. Yeah we were bad, but if anything things seem to be getting worse. A few of us had knives back then, now it is knives *and* guns on the streets of many towns and cities. I put it down to things such as rap music, having no father figure and nothing to keep some young people occupied.

But what can you do to save the streets, to change the youths? Nobody could have saved me. I had to save myself, and some people will never do that. They are the ones who carry on a life of petty crime, never being successful, always in and out of jail. And once you are in that cycle it is so hard to break out of it. But anything that helps is good. So I hope people will use my book to try and get inside the mind-set of street kids.

Now in amongst all this darkness a pretty little thing touched my world and started to bring sunshine and stability into it—my daughter, the single best thing to ever enter my life. When I look at her I feel unconditional love and that is one of the best feelings, oh yeah and fear, worry, anxiety and all the rest that goes with it on her behalf. Having a child was some scary stuff. At first I couldn't handle the responsibility. I ran like a lot of men do and never bonded with her until she was about one-year-old. She has grown into this little thing that literally melts my heart. When I give her a hug all the past is erased. It isn't about me anymore it is about her, providing a happy and stable childhood for my princess. By my own efforts, I'm a writer, I have a nice family, a nice car, a nice home, and I have some real friends, that is what life is about.

You may have a book inside you. You may have pain and anger deep inside. Once it gets bottled up the bottle may eventually explode, and the anger and pain come out in negative ways. Talking to somebody about your issues releases the hurt, the pain, the fears. Never be ashamed to talk, we all have things we need to get off our chest. I had a year of therapy, one of the best moves I ever made. I went into that first session a depressed young man walking the streets with my dog, both of us with our heads down. A year later I left as a devoted father, training at the gym, with a whole new set of friends, finding happiness and stability. I haven't looked back since.

All of you doctors that throw medication at the vulnerable, take a leaf out of my book. I was drugged up to the eyeballs whilst in prison, and when the drugs wore off the problems were still there for all to see. Therapy and bodybuilding did it for me. It doesn't have to be lifting dumbbells, or doing pull-ups. Exercise is good for the mind, it brings happy vibes to the brain. If you have a self-destructive personality then forget the drink and the drugs. Swap these for a gym and a good diet, a healthy body and a healthy mind. These are the things that changed me, and maybe it can change a few other people. Everyone has to find their own way.

Forget, 'Oh I'm gonna do this or that one day'. Get up off your arse and do it now! I never said, 'I *might* write a book' or 'My book *might* get published'.

I said, 'I *will* write about my life and it *will be* published'. This self-control and positive energy has saved me in all sorts of ways, and gets me to where I am going. Forget sympathy, the world doesn't owe you or me anything. It is up to each of us to get up and change our own little world, our own bubble, our own future. Don't waste years like I did. Go with your instinct. Make your mark. Oh yeah, and one more thing, try to live your life so that you don't look back with regret.

From a lost boy to a found man.

Justin Rollins

January 2011

INDEX

snooker cue *65*

Stanley knife *48*

superglue *124*

weirdos *141*

welfare *157*

Whitemoor Prison *152*

wild child *65*

Wimbledon *30, 42, 52, 77, 95, 126*

Wimbledon Magistrates' Court *133*

Wimbledon Police Station *44, 45, 117, 124, 129*

Wimbledon Youth Court *45*

wimps *55*

windows

breaking windows *57*

winners *158*

WK (Who Kares/Wanted Kriminals) *32, 47, 48, 87, 113*

WK towns *52*

Woolwich *110*

Worcester Park *17, 52, 61*

work *112*

working-class system *111*

Wormword Scrubs *131*

worry *159*

Y

young offender *141*

young offenders *132, 134*

young offender unit *135*

young offender unit *136, 137, 145*

youth offending team *78*

Z

Zelda *42, 43*

The Geese Theatre Handbook
Drama with Offenders and People at Risk

Edited by Clark Baim, Sally Brookes
and Alun Mountford

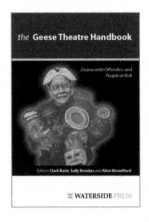

Geese Theatre UK is renowned across the criminal
justice field. Members of the company devise and
perform issue-based plays and conduct workshops
and training in prisons, young offender institutions, probation centres and related settings. The
company has worked in virtually every prison
and each probation area in the UK and Ireland
— and also works with youth offending teams.

The Geese Theatre Handbook explains the thinking behind the
company's approach to applied drama with offenders and people at risk of offending, including young people.

- Contains 100+ exercises with explanations, instructions and suggestions
- Helps practitioners develop their own style and approach
- Materials can be readily adapted to other settings including con-
  flict resolution, restorative justice and interpersonal skills training.

'An invaluable resource': ***Prison Service News***

'An absolute treasure trove for people who work with groups - in mental
health, schools, training, social work - wherever': ***Mental Health Today***

'A generous book [which] provides a treasure chest of games and exercise for
any group setting . . . a wealth of food for thought . . . for trainers of all kinds
. . . an invaluable addition to the Waterside list': ***Criminal Justice Matters***

ISBN 9781872870670 (Paperback) 9781906534509 (Ebook) | 2002 | 224 pages

Nipping Crime in the Bud
How the Philanthropic Quest Was Put Into Law

by Muriel Whitten, Foreword by Rob Allen

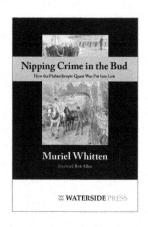

Uniquely, the book traces the first hard won policy
networks and partnerships between government and
the voluntary sector. It reveals how—sometimes
against the odds, with funding on a knife edge but
constantly striving for effective answers—influ-
ential philanthropists rose to the challenge and
changed approaches to young people involved in
crime and delinquency, traces of which endure
today within the great crime prevention charities which still rally to this cause.

Muriel Whitten's book draws on previously neglected archival sources and other
first-hand research to create a formidable and illuminating account about what,
for many people, will be a missing chapter in English social and legal history.

'Describes in colourful detail the background to the founding of the Society and
how its founders and their successors worked. It explains how their plans were
put into practice, how they governed and how they acquired support. It skil-
fully deals with questions that are still asked today such as to what extent are
children to be held responsible for wrongdoing? ... Dr Whitten is admirably
suited to write such a book ... [and] her knowledge and experience are distilled
in this comprehensive and well-written title': **John Hostettler, legal historian.**

ISBN 9781872870658 (Paperback) 9781906534981 (Ebook) | Nov 2010 | 300 pages

WatersidePress.co.uk

'When Mr Weaver talks about the importance of tackling the causes of crime, he does so from an unusual position of authority and experience': *The Scotsman*

So You Think You Know Me?
by Allan Weaver
Foreword by Mike Nellis and Fergus McNeill

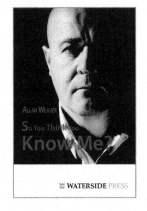

The autobiography of an ex-offender and twice-times inmate of Barlinnie Prison, now a social work team-leader in his native Scotland.

As a local hard case, author Allan Weaver took no prisoners. Neither does he in this compelling work in which he tells of a life of violent episodes and his chaotic early life. Teachers, social workers and 'authority figures' never tried 'to get to know him' to unearth the clues and triggers and discover what his offending was all about. A natural rebel and a radical, it is hardly surprising that by ignoring the real Allan Weaver this led to an escalation of his violent activities, tensions between family and friends and dubious associates.

So You Think You Know Me? is packed with contradictions: the Allan Weaver involved in mayhem and aggression is not the one telling the story from inside his own head: an often vulnerable, sensitive, articulate, unquestionably loyal and even-handed individual; mistaken, misguided and foolish perhaps but largely trapped by an increasing need to live up to his 'tough guy' reputation.

'Despite all the tribulations he faced in his early life Weaver conveys his experiences with humour and affection. I thoroughly recommend this book to anyone who wants to be reminded of why they embarked on a career in the probation service': ***Probation Journal***

ISBN 9781904380450 (Paperback) 9781906534714 (Ebook) | June 2008 | 224 pages

Lightning Source UK Ltd.
Milton Keynes UK
UKOW04f2308101017
310752UK00002B/203/P